Advancing Excellence in Technological Literacy:
Student Assessment, Professional Development, and Program Standards

Companion to—*Standards for Technological Literacy:
Content for the Study of Technology*
International Technology Education Association
and its Technology for All Americans Project

The International Technology Education Association and its Technology for All Americans Project developed *Advancing Excellence in Technological Literacy: Student Assessment, Professional Development, and Program Standards* through funding from the National Science Foundation under Grant No. ESI-0000897 and the National Aeronautics and Space Administration under Grant No. NCC5-519. Any opinions, findings, and conclusions or recommendations expressed in this material are those of the author(s) and do not necessarily reflect the views of the National Science Foundation or the National Aeronautics and Space Administration.

ISBN: 1-887101-03-9

Copies of this document are being distributed by the
International Technology Education Association
1914 Association Drive, Suite 201
Reston, Virginia 20191-1539
Phone: (703) 860-2100
Fax: (703) 860-0353
Email: itea@iris.org
URL: www.iteawww.org

Contents

Preface

Advancing Excellence in Technological Literacy: Student Assessment, Professional Development, and Program Standards (*AETL*) is a companion document to *Standards for Technological Literacy: Content for the Study of Technology* (*STL*). Specifically, it presents standards and enabling guidelines for student assessment, professional development of teachers, and the program infrastructure associated with the study of technology in Grades K–12. *AETL* is a valuable resource to promote technological literacy for all students.

AETL was developed by the International Technology Education Association's Technology for All Americans Project (ITEA-TfAAP) by way of generous support from the National Science Foundation (NSF) and the National Aeronautics and Space Administration (NASA) from 2000–2003. Many people assisted with the development and refinement of this document. Valuable input was provided by the ITEA-TfAAP Advisory Group, the Standards Writing Team, the Standards Specialists, the ITEA Board of Directors, and various focus groups. We would like to express our appreciation to NSF, NASA, and everyone involved in formulating this document (see Appendix B).

AETL will be useful to all persons interested in seeing that students are technologically literate as a result of formal education. We are optimistic about the contribution *AETL* will make as a companion document to *STL*. Together, these publications provide direction for the study of technology by delineating requirements for student assessment, professional development of teacher candidates and existing teachers, and program enhancement for the study of technology. The standards and guidelines in this document will help professionals in education ensure that all students achieve technological literacy.

William E. Dugger, Jr., DTE
Director
Technology for All Americans Project
International Technology
Education Association

Michael D. Wright, DTE
President
International Technology
Education Association

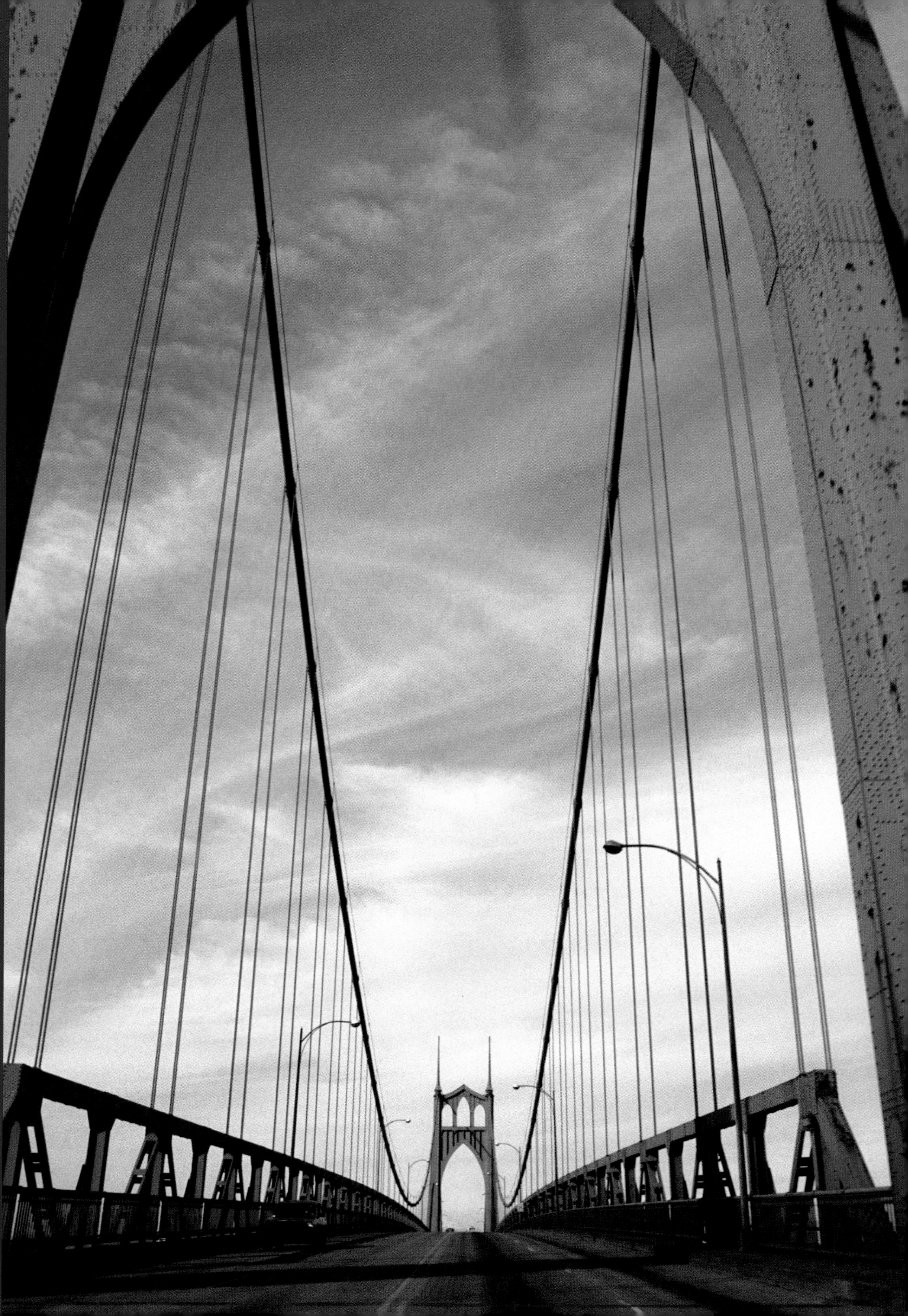

CHAPTER 1

Overview of *Advancing Excellence in Technological Literacy*

I n 2000, the International Technology Education Association (ITEA), through its Technology for All Americans Project (TfAAP), released *Standards for Technological Literacy: Content for the Study of Technology* (STL) (ITEA, 2000a). Funding for TfAAP was made available through the National Science Foundation (NSF) and the National Aeronautics and Space Administration (NASA). *STL* provides a significant foundational basis for the study of technology in terms of content, but it is not enough.

Advancing Excellence in Technological Literacy: Student Assessment, Professional Development, and Program Standards (AETL) is vital because *STL* alone cannot make sufficient educational reform in the study of technology. The two documents should enjoy a symbiotic relationship: *STL* validates *AETL*, and clear alignment between *AETL* and *STL* upholds the content standards. The purpose of *AETL* is to facilitate technological literacy for all students.

Rationale

We live in a technological world. Living in the twenty-first century requires much more from every individual than a basic ability to read, write, and perform simple mathematics. Technology affects virtually every aspect of our lives, from enabling citizens to perform routine tasks to requiring that they be able to make responsible, informed decisions that affect individuals, our society, and the environment.

Technology has enhanced human communications, comfort, safety, productivity, medical care, and agriculture, among many other things. However, the world is affected by both natural problems and problems that arise from the human modification of the natural world. Examples of these include arctic warming, overpopulation, escalating drought, elevated carbon emissions, unregulated deforestation, and the deterioration of coral reefs. On one hand, tech-

The purpose of *AETL* is to facilitate technological literacy for all students.

nology has added to the degradation of the natural environment while on the other hand, technology is viewed by many as a panacea to solve these and future problems. It is imperative that we prepare a more technologically literate citizenry that is knowledgeable and able to comprehend such problems.

Citizens of today must have a basic understanding of how technology affects their world and how they exist both within and around technology. The need for technological literacy is as fundamentally important to students as traditional core subject area knowledge and abilities. Students need and deserve the opportunity to attain technological literacy through the educational process.

Standards for Technological Literacy

Technological literacy is the ability to use, manage, assess, and understand technology.

The vision of achieving technological literacy for all students is a fundamental principle of *STL*. The content standards (see Appendix C) and related benchmarks identify what all students need to know and be able to do to progress toward technological literacy. *STL* provides the content basis upon which the study of technology may be built. It does not, however, address such important topics as student assessment, professional development, and program enhancement.

Features of Advancing Excellence in Technological Literacy

Technology is the innovation, change, or modification of the natural environment to satisfy perceived human needs and wants.

AETL was created to provide the means for implementing *STL* in K–12 laboratory-classrooms. Chapter 2 discusses principles and related definitions that are relevant to this document. *AETL* consists of three separate but interrelated sets of standards:

- Chapter 3: Student Assessment Standards
- Chapter 4: Professional Development Standards
- Chapter 5: Program Standards

The standards in *AETL* are based upon *STL*. To fully and effectively implement the content standards in *STL*, all of the *AETL* standards presented in chapters 3, 4, and 5 must be met through the guidelines. Users should read this document comprehensively. (See Table 1 for the number of standards and guidelines in *AETL*.)

Table 1. The Number of Standards and Guidelines in *AETL*

AETL Sets of Standards	Standards	Guidelines	
Student Assessment	5	23	
Professional Development	7	36	
Program	5	24	30

AETL is designed to leave specific curricular decisions to teachers, schools, school districts, and states/provinces/regions. *STL* and *AETL* describe the attributes of the effective study of technology that lead to technological literacy. Teachers, professional development providers, and administrators should use *STL* and *AETL* as guides for advancing technological literacy for all students.

AETL also includes:

- Chapter 6: Achieving the Vision by Working Together
- Appendices

Chapter 6 invites users to participate in the visionary basis of *STL* and *AETL*. The appendices include a history of TfAAP (Appendix A), acknowledgements (Appendix B), a listing of content standards for technological literacy (Appendix C), a listing of the standards and guidelines from *AETL* (Appendix D), a correlation chart (Appendix E), references and resources (Appendix F), a glossary (Appendix G), and an index (Appendix H). The glossary terms are provided for clarity of intention within this document.

Chapter 3: Student Assessment Standards

Chapter 3 presents criteria for teachers to use in judging the quality of student assessment practices. The standards are applicable to those who educate students on any aspect of technology. The five organizational topics for the student assessment standards are:

- Consistency with *STL*
- Intended Purpose
- Research-Based Assessment Principles
- Practical Contexts
- Data Collection

The student assessment standards define how assessment of technological literacy should be designed and implemented, but the chapter does not lay out an assessment

> **Table 2. Student Assessment Standards**
>
> A-1. Assessment of student learning will be consistent with *Standards for Technological Literacy: Content for the Study of Technology (STL)*.
> A-2. Assessment of student learning will be explicitly matched to the intended purpose.
> A-3. Assessment of student learning will be systematic and derived from research-based assessment principles.
> A-4. Assessment of student learning will reflect practical contexts consistent with the nature of technology.
> A-5. Assessment of student learning will incorporate data collection for accountability, professional development, and program enhancement.

tool—that is, it does not provide a test, quiz, or other handy instrument to be photocopied and used in the laboratory-classroom. This task is left—as it should be—to individual teachers and others.

Users of the student assessment standards should recognize that student assessment should be *formative* (ongoing) as well as *summative* (occurring at the end). Further, users should recognize that the assessment process should be ***informative***; that is, it should inform students and teachers about progress toward technological literacy and provide data on the effectiveness of instruction and programs. Teachers should use student assessment data to improve classroom practices, plan curricula, develop self-directed learners, report student progress, and research teaching practices. Student assessment data provide information to policymakers on the success of the policies that have been implemented.

Student assessment refers to the systematic, multi-step process of collecting evidence on student learning, understanding, and abilities and using that information to inform instruction and provide feedback to the learner, thereby enhancing student learning.

The standards presented in chapter 3 (see Table 2) relate only to student assessment. Evaluation of professional development is found in chapter 4, and evaluation of programs is found in chapter 5.

Chapter 4: Professional Development Standards

Chapter 4 presents criteria for professional development providers (including teacher educators, supervisors, and administrators) to use in planning professional development. The standards are applicable to those who prepare teachers on any aspect of technology. The seven organizational topics for the professional development standards are:

- Consistency with *STL*
- Students as Learners
- Curricula and Programs
- Instructional Strategies
- Learning Environments
- Continued Professional Growth
- Pre-Service and In-Service

Professional development providers who organize pre-service and in-service education need to revise their curricula and teaching methodologies to align with *STL* and *AETL*. Technology is a continuously changing field of study, and teachers must be well prepared with the ability and motivation to stay informed and current on technological advances throughout their careers. Consequently, becoming an effective teacher is a continuous process of life-

Table 3. Professional Development Standards
PD-1. Professional development will provide teachers with knowledge, abilities, and understanding consistent with *Standards for Technological Literacy: Content for the Study of Technology* (*STL*).
PD-2. Professional development will provide teachers with educational perspectives on students as learners of technology.
PD-3. Professional development will prepare teachers to design and evaluate technology curricula and programs.
PD-4. Professional development will prepare teachers to use instructional strategies that enhance technology teaching, student learning, and student assessment.
PD-5. Professional development will prepare teachers to design and manage learning environments that promote technological literacy.
PD-6. Professional development will prepare teachers to be responsible for their own continued professional growth.
PD-7. Professional development providers will plan, implement, and evaluate the pre-service and in-service education of teachers.

long learning and growth that begins early in life, continues through the undergraduate, pre-service experience, and extends through the in-service years. Users of this document should focus on preparing teachers to continue to pursue professional development to keep up with changing technologies and current research on how students learn.

Many states/provinces/regions are experiencing a shortage of qualified, licensed technology teachers. Therefore, a quality professional development program based on the professional development standards (see Table 3) is essential. Faculty members in every teacher preparation program should address *STL* and *AETL* to determine how the technological literacy of teacher candidates can be enhanced. The necessity to address issues of technological literacy is pertinent to all programs that prepare teachers of every grade level, including K–5 elementary teachers and teachers of science, mathematics, social studies, language arts, and other content areas.

Chapter 5: Program Standards

Chapter 5 presents criteria for teachers and administrators (including supervisors) responsible for technology programs. The standards are applicable to those who organize the learning of students on any aspect of technology. The five organizational topics for the program standards are:

- Consistency with *STL*
- Implementation
- Evaluation
- Learning Environments
- Management

Users of the program standards should recognize that thoughtful design and implementation of programs for the study of technology are necessary to provide comprehensive and coordinated experiences for all students across grade levels and disciplines. Coordinated experiences result in effective learning; accordingly the program standards must be synchronized with the content standards (*STL*) as well as with the student assessment and professional development standards in *AETL*. The study of technology should be developmentally appropriate for every student, and it should be coordinated with other school subjects, including science, mathematics, social studies, language arts, and other content areas.

> **Program refers to everything that affects student learning, including content, professional development, curricula, instruction, student assessment, and the learning environment, implemented across grade levels.**

Table 4. Program Standards

P-1. Technology program development will be consistent with *Standards for Technological Literacy: Content for the Study of Technology* (*STL*).

P-2. Technology program implementation will facilitate technological literacy for all students.

P-3. Technology program evaluation will ensure and facilitate technological literacy for all students.

P-4. Technology program learning environments will facilitate technological literacy for all students.

P-5. Technology program management will be provided by designated personnel at the school, school district, and state/provincial/regional levels.

The program standards (see Table 4) call for extending programs for the study of technology beyond the domain of the school. Programs should, for example, involve parents, the community, business and industry, school-to-work programs, and higher education as well as professionals in engineering and other careers related to technology. And finally, it is essential that adequate support for professional development be provided by administrators to ensure that teachers remain current with the evolving fields of technology and educational research.

Advancing Excellence in Technological Literacy: Student Assessment, Professional Development, and Program Standards

Sample Standard with Guidelines and Sample Vignette

The format for a sample standard with guidelines and a sample vignette can be found in Figure 1.

Figure 1. Format of a Sample Standard with Guidelines and a Sample Vignette

Standards (in large bold type) describe what should be done by the user. They are identified by prefixes such as *A* for student assessment, *PD* for professional development, and *P* for program.

Narratives of Standards explain what is included in the standards and why they are important.

Guidelines (in smaller bold type) state specific requirements or enablers that identify what needs to be done in order to meet the standard.

Narratives of Guidelines provide further elaboration and examples of the guidelines.

Notations consist of definitions, tables, quotations, and correlations. The correlations show connections within and between the standards in *AETL* and *STL*.

Vignettes give ideas or examples of how standards can be implemented.

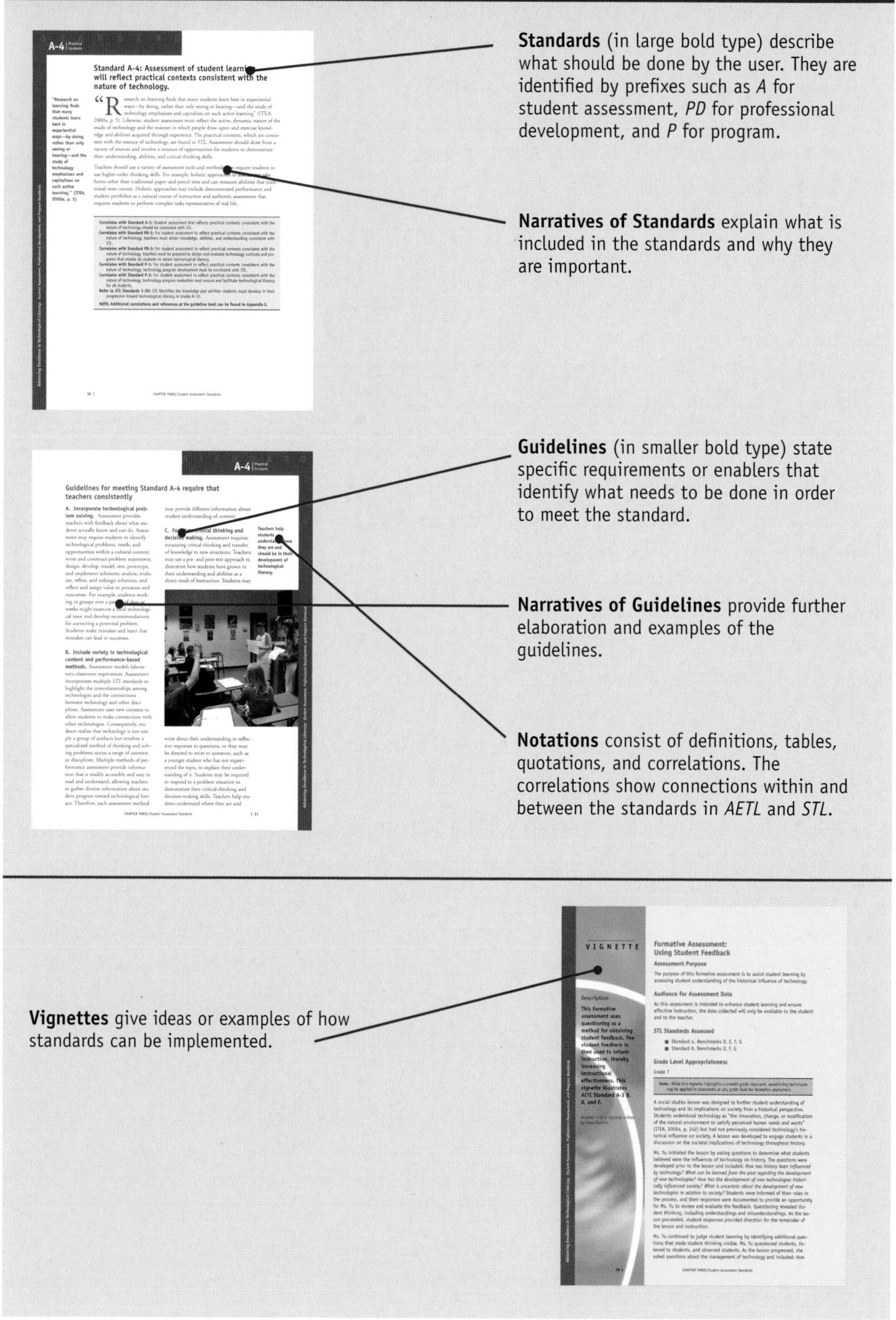

Architecture of a Standard

Standards, which are statements about what is valued that can be used for making a judgment of quality, are in sentence form in bold type. The standards are relatively large in font size, as they represent a fundamental concept.

Note that each standard is identified by a prefix letter and number (e.g., P-4). Student assessment standards are identified by the letter *A*, professional development standards are identified by the letters *PD*, and program standards are identified by the letter *P*. Each standard is further identified by a number; however, this does not imply a sequential or ranking order. All of the standards are of equal importance. In other words, PD-5 is of equal importance to PD-1 or PD-3. The goal is to meet all of the standards in each chapter.

Narrative of a Standard

A narrative follows each standard and explains the intent of the standard, including possible applications of the standard by the user.

Architecture of a Guideline

Under each standard a number of guidelines are presented and must be addressed to enable the user to meet a given standard. **ITEA does not recommend that users eliminate any of the guidelines; however, users may add to the guidelines if there is a need to accommodate local differences.**

Guidelines are printed in bold type and are identified by a capital letter prefix such as *A, B, C*, etc. "Stem" statements appear before the guidelines are specified and should be used when quoting individual guidelines. Stem statements connect individual guidelines to the context of the standard.

Narrative of a Guideline

Each guideline is followed by a supporting narrative that provides further detail, clarity, and examples.

Notations

Notations consist of definitions, tables, quotations, and correlations. Definitions are provided to offer further explanation or emphasis. Tables provide details or data relevant to *AETL*. Correlations identify the relationships within and between student assessment, professional development, and program standards and are provided to increase the usability of *AETL*. The intent of such referencing is to identify connections among standards. In addition, *STL* is referenced as a means for illustrating correlations between *STL* and *AETL*. Some correlations are inserted in the text of chapters 3, 4, and 5 immediately following the standard narratives. Further, Appendix E is a chart that lists all of these correlations as well as additional correlations at the guideline level.

> A standard is a written statement about what is valued that can be used for making a judgment of quality.

> The goal is to meet all of the standards in each chapter.

> A guideline is a specific requirement or enabler that identifies what needs to be done in order to meet a standard.

> Stem statements appear before guidelines to connect them to the standard addressed. Stem statements should always be used when quoting individual guidelines.

Advancing Excellence in Technological Literacy: Student Assessment, Professional Development, and Program Standards

Vignettes

Vignettes, by nature, provide "snapshots" of what may happen in student assessment, professional development, or programs and are located in chapters 3, 4, and 5. They provide detailed examples of how the standards can be put into practice. Some of the vignettes are authentic, having been successfully used in laboratory-classrooms. A few of the vignettes were generated especially for *AETL* and are fictional, not having been tried and tested. Users should be cautioned not to read any vignette too literally or narrowly.

Redundancy of the Standards

Although the three sets of standards in *AETL* are presented in three separate chapters, they are broadly overlapping in nature. For example, professional development must address both student assessment and program enhancement. Likewise, programs must incorporate the elements of both student assessment and professional development. As with other standards documents, *AETL* should be viewed as dynamic and open to review, revision, and improvement.

Designing the Future

STL sets forth the vision that all students can become technologically literate. To realize this vision, *STL* and *AETL* must be implemented. This will take considerable time and effort, but the rewards will be worthwhile in terms of personal, national, and global achievement: a populace that has knowledge and abilities to understand how human innovation can modify the world and universe in positive and productive ways.

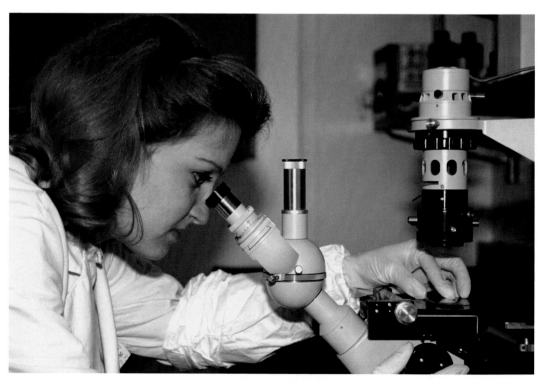

Principles and Related Definitions

A Gallup poll on "What Americans Think About Technology" (Rose & Dugger, 2002) revealed that while adults in the United States are very interested in technology, they are relatively uninformed about technology. Using a National Science Foundation (NSF) grant, the International Technology Education Association (ITEA) commissioned the Gallup Organization in the spring of 2001 to research American citizens' knowledge and abilities pursuant to technological literacy. Content established in *Standards for Technological Literacy: Content for the Study of Technology (STL)* (ITEA, 2000a) provided the foundational basis for the 17 questions used in the survey. It revealed the public's definition of technology to be very narrow when compared to the opinions of national experts in the fields of technology, engineering, and science. When provided with a more accepted, encompassing definition of technology, however, American citizens nearly unanimously supported the need for technological literacy. Moreover, they strongly supported the study of technology in schools as a means to increase technological literacy for all people.

What is Technological Literacy?

ITEA's *STL* defines technological literacy as the ability to use, manage, assess, and understand technology. More specifically

1. The ability to use technology involves the successful operation of the systems of the time. This includes knowing the components of existing macrosystems and human adaptive systems and knowing how the systems behave.
2. The ability to manage technology involves ensuring that all technological activities are efficient and appropriate.
3. Assessing involves being able to make judgments and decisions about technology on an informed basis rather than an emotional one.

Advancing Excellence in Technological Literacy: Student Assessment, Professional Development, and Program Standards

4. Understanding technology involves the ability to understand and synthesize facts and information into new insights (ITEA, 1996).

From a related perspective, a publication prepared by the National Academy of Engineering (NAE) and the National Research Council (NRC) entitled *Technically Speaking: Why All Americans Need to Know More About Technology* (2002), states that "technological literacy encompasses three interdependent dimensions—knowledge, ways of thinking and acting, and capabilities. Like literacy in science, mathematics, social studies, or language arts, the goal of technological literacy is to provide people with the tools to participate intelligently and thoughtfully in the world around them" (p. 3).

Technological literacy, like other forms of literacy, is what *every person* needs in order to be an informed and contributing citizen for the world of today and tomorrow. Therefore students, to achieve technological literacy, must develop a broad range of technological knowledge and abilities. On the other hand, technological competency is what *some* people need to be prepared to be successful in a technical career. Teachers must be technologically competent to direct student learning.

What is Technology?

How can technology best be defined? *STL* defines technology as "the innovation, change, or modification of the natural environment in order to satisfy perceived human wants and needs" (ITEA, 2000a, p. 242). This is compatible with the definition provided in the *National Science Education Standards*, which states, ". . . the goal of technology is to make modifications in the world to meet human needs" (NRC, 1996, p. 24). Parallel to these definitions, the American Association for the Advancement of Science's (AAAS) *Benchmarks for Science Literacy* presents the following: "In the broadest sense, technology extends our abilities to change the world: to cut, shape, or put together materials; to move things from one place to another; to reach farther with our hands, voices, and senses" (1993, p. 41). In the NAE and NRC publication, *Technically Speaking*, technology is described as ". . . the process by which humans modify nature to meet their needs and wants" (2002, p. 2). All four of these definitions of technology are very similar and reinforce each other.

What is the Study of Technology?

Schools that encourage the study of technology provide all students with concepts and experiences necessary to develop understanding and abilities for the constantly changing technological world (ITEA, 1996). The study of technology enhances student learning by highlighting the relationships among technologies and between technology and other school subjects, including science, mathematics, social studies, language arts, and other content areas (ITEA, 2000a). Students are engaged in activities that promote technological literacy through the development of knowledge and abilities necessary to make informed decisions regarding the use and management of technology. The study of technology is comprehensive, incorporating content identified in *STL*. Technology teachers and other content area teachers provide learning opportunities that focus on the content in *STL*. The study of technology begins in kindergarten and progresses through Grade 12, providing continuous learning opportunities to students.

While the study of technology occurs in a continuous, cross-curricular fashion, it is also promoted in classrooms specifically charged to develop technologically literate students. Technology education plays a crucial role in advancing students toward technological literacy. Students engage in cognitive and psychomotor activities that foster critical thinking, decision making, and problem solving related to the use, management, and evaluation of the designed world.

Technology education is not the same as *educational technology*. Sometimes referred to as instructional technology, educational technology involves using technological developments, such as computers, audiovisual equipment, and mass media, as tools to enhance and optimize the teaching and learning environment in all school subjects, including technology education. *Technology education*, however, is a school subject specifically designed to help students develop technological literacy.

The student assessment, professional development, and program standards provided in *AETL* were developed to facilitate technological literacy for all students. At the elementary level, the implementation of *STL* and *AETL* will be a major responsibility of the regular classroom teacher. At the middle and high school levels, technology teachers facilitate technological literacy learning in dedicated technology laboratory-classrooms. Teachers of other content areas should receive professional development to allow them to incorporate the content in *STL* and *AETL* into their teaching as appropriate. For programs to effectively support technological literacy for all students, elementary teachers, technology teachers, and other content area teachers must work together to realize the vision of *STL* and *AETL*.

Characteristics of a Technologically Literate Person

Technologically literate people are problem solvers who consider technological issues from different points of view and relate them to a variety of contexts. They understand technological impacts and consequences, acknowledging that the solution to one problem may create other problems. They also understand that solutions often involve trade-offs, which necessitate accepting less of one quality in order to gain more of another. They appreciate the interrelationships between technology and individuals, society, and the environment. *Technically Speaking* states, "Technological literacy is more of a capacity to understand the broader technological world rather than an ability to work with specific pieces of it" (NAE & NRC, 2002, p. 22).

Technologically literate people understand that technology involves systems, which are groups of interrelated components designed to collectively achieve a desired goal or goals. No single component, device, or process can be considered without understanding its relationships to all other components, devices, and processes in the system. Those who are technologically literate have the ability to use concepts from science, mathematics, social studies, language arts, and other content areas as tools for understanding

The study of technology is any formal or informal education about human innovation, change, or modification of the natural environment.

Technology education is NOT the same as educational technology.

"Technological literacy is more of a capacity to understand the broader technological world rather than an ability to work with specific pieces of it." (NAE & NRC, 2002, p. 22)

and managing technological systems. Therefore, technologically literate people use a strong systems-oriented, creative, and productive approach to thinking about and solving technological problems.

Technologically literate people can identify appropriate solutions and assess and forecast the results of implementing the chosen solution. They understand the major technological concepts behind current issues and appreciate the importance of fundamental technological developments. They are skilled in the safe use of technological processes that may be prerequisites for their careers, health, or enjoyment. Most importantly, technologically literate people understand that technology is the result of human activity (ITEA, 1996).

Why is Technological Literacy Important?

Several groups, organizations, agencies, and institutions have made the case for technological literacy, including ITEA (1996, 2000a; Rose & Dugger, 2002) as well as NAE and NRC (2002). As the U.S. Commission on National Security/21st Century reported in 2001: "The health of the U.S. economy . . . will depend not only on [science, math, and engineering] professionals but also on a populace that can effectively assimilate a wide range of new tools and technologies" (p. 39).

The results of the ITEA Gallup Poll indicate a very narrow view of technology by the American public, who define it as primarily computers and the Internet. A number of questions in the poll focused on the study of technology and technological literacy as a part of the school curriculum. When provided with a definition of technology more accepted by experts in the field, nearly all of the respondents (97%) agreed that schools should include the study of technology in the curriculum. Of those 97%, over half said that they thought the study of technology should be required as a school subject. The public believes technological literacy should be a part of high school graduation requirements.

How widespread is technological literacy among Americans today? Unfortunately, no definitive research exists on this topic. Levels of technological literacy vary from person to person and depend upon backgrounds, education, interests, attitudes, and abilities. Many people are not prepared to perform routine technological activities or appreciate the significance of engineering breakthroughs.

The study of technology has traditionally not been accepted as a core subject area requirement in many elementary, middle, and high schools. For most individuals, technological literacy has been traditionally gained through daily activities. However, technological processes and systems have become so complex that the happenstance approach is no longer effective. A massive, coordinated effort is needed in order to achieve a technologically literate populace. This should involve schools, mass media and entertainment outlets, book publishers, and museums. Schools, in collaboration with the community, must bear the bulk of this effort, because the educational system can provide the most comprehensive study of technology.

Other Relevant Definitions

The principal discipline being advocated in this document is technology, which is closely related to science, mathematics, and engineering. Science, which deals with ". . . understand[ing] the natural world" (NRC, 1996, p. 24), is the underpinning of technology. Science is concerned with "what is" in the natural world, while technology deals with "what can be" invented, innovated, or designed from the natural world. Rodger Bybee, President of Biological Sciences Curriculum Study (BSCS), explains:

> The lack of technological literacy is compounded by one prevalent misconception. When asked to define technology, most individuals reply with the archaic, and mostly erroneous, idea that technology is applied science. Although this definition of technology has a long standing in this country, it is well past time to establish a new understanding about technology . . . it is in the interest of science, science education, and society to help students and all citizens develop a greater understanding and appreciation for some of the fundamental concepts and processes of technology and engineering. (2000, pp. 23–24)

"Mathematics is the science of patterns and relationships" (AAAS, 1993, p. 23). It provides an exact language for technology, science, and engineering. Developments in technology, such as the computer, stimulate mathematics, just as developments in mathematics often enhance innovations in technology. One example of this is mathematical modeling that can assist technological design by simulating how a proposed system may operate.

"Engineering is the profession in which a knowledge of the mathematical and natural sciences gained by study, experience, and practice is applied with judgment to develop ways to utilize economically the materials and forces of nature for the benefit of mankind" (Accreditation Board for Engineering and Technology [ABET], 2002, back cover). There are strong philosophical connections between the disciplines of technology and engineering. The engineering profession has begun to work with technology teachers to develop alliances for infusing engineering concepts into K–12 education. The alliances will provide a mechanism for greater appreciation and understanding of engineering and technology. The National Academy of Engineering is an avid supporter of technological literacy.

Definitions Related to Education

Many times in documents such as this, educational terms like *program, content, professional development, curricula, instruction, student assessment, learning environment, student learning*, and others are presented without definition. In hopes of providing a better understanding of these terms as they relate to the study of technology, some specific meanings are provided here as well as in the Glossary (Appendix G).

The term *program* is a large and all-encompassing term in education. In this document, program refers to everything that affects student learning, including content, professional development, curricula, instruction, student assessment, and the learning environment, implemented across grade levels. For example, a middle school technology

Science deals with ". . . understand[ing] the natural world." (NRC, 1996, p. 24)

"Mathematics is the science of patterns and relationships." (AAAS, 1993, p. 23)

"Engineering is the profession in which a knowledge of the mathematical and natural sciences gained by study, experience, and practices is applied with judgments to develop ways to utilize economically the materials and forces of nature for the benefit of mankind." (ABET, 2002, back cover)

Advancing Excellence in Technological Literacy: Student Assessment, Professional Development, and Program Standards

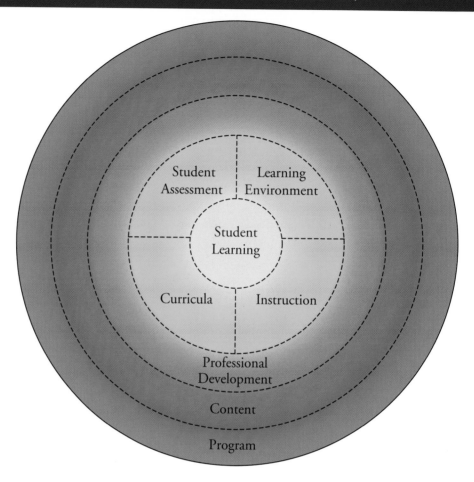

Figure 2. Graphic Model of Selected Components in a Middle School Technology Program (Grades 6–8)

Student Assessment

Learning Environment

Student Learning

Curricula

Instruction

Professional Development

Content

Program

program would include everything that affects student learning in Grades 6–8 in a school or school district. A graphic model of selected components in a middle school technology program is shown in Figure 2.

Programs for the study of technology support student attainment of technological literacy through technology programs as well as other content area programs. In other words, programs for the study of technology are cross-curricular in nature. The technology program incorporates the study of technology across grade levels as a core subject of inherent value. The cross-curricular technology program manages the study of technology across grade levels and disciplines.

In the study of technology, the program encompasses the *content*, which delineates the cognitive knowledge and tactile abilities students should learn in order to become technologically literate. Content may be viewed as the subject-matter ingredients that go into the curriculum. The content for the study of technology is provided in *STL*.

Professional development is a continuous process of lifelong learning and growth that begins early in life, continues through the undergraduate, pre-service experience, and extends through the in-service years. For program content to be aligned with *STL*, teachers must have access to professional development.

Curricula are the way the content is delivered each day in laboratory-classrooms. Curricula include the structure, organization, balance, and presentation of the content to the student and provide the plan followed by the teacher for instruction. *STL* is not a curriculum.

Instruction is the actual teaching process used by the teacher to deliver the content to all students. It involves various teaching methods, strategies, and techniques (e.g., lectures, questioning, demonstrations, etc.). Instruction also requires an understanding of how students learn.

Student assessment refers to the systematic, multi-step process of collecting evidence on student learning, understanding, and abilities and using that information to inform instruction and provide feedback to the learner, thereby enhancing student learning. In order to collect data in some quantifiable manner, the process of measurement is employed.

The *learning environment* is the place where instruction occurs. It could be a classroom or a laboratory, or it could be a non-conventional location, such as a museum, a business or industry, or an outdoor location. The learning environment consists of such things as space, equipment, resources (including supplies and materials), and safety and health requirements.

The primary purpose of the program is to facilitate and enhance *student learning* (see Figure 2). Content, professional development, curricula, instruction, student assessment, and the learning environment must be coordinated for student learning to be effective.

Summary

Technological literacy is imperative for the twenty-first century. Employing technology, humans have changed the world. Understanding the symbiotic relationships between technology and science, mathematics, social studies, language arts, and other content areas is vital for the future. The principles and definitions presented in this chapter are intended to help the user better comprehend the standards presented in this document. *STL* and *AETL* provide many of the tools necessary to reform technology programs to ensure efficiency and effectiveness. *AETL* (student assessment, professional development, and program), along with *STL* (content), provides guidance for improving student learning and provides direction for the future study of technology.

AETL, along with STL, provides guidance for improving student learning and provides direction for the future study of technology.

Advancing Excellence in Technological Literacy: Student Assessment, Professional Development, and Program Standards

Student Assessment Standards

The standards in this chapter describe effective and appropriate technological literacy assessment practices to be used by teachers and by local, district, state/provincial/regional, and national/federal entities. These assessment standards are based on *Standards for Technological Literacy: Content for the Study of Technology* (STL) (ITEA, 2000a). They are intended to be implemented in conjunction with *STL* as well as with the professional development and program standards included in *Advancing Excellence in Technological Literacy: Student Assessment, Professional Development, and Program Standards* (AETL). Therefore, these standards are of optimal use when curriculum and instruction have incorporated the concepts and principles identified in *STL*; accordingly, **these standards apply to assessment of student technological literacy in any K–12 classroom**, not just within technology laboratory-classrooms.

In designing assessment tools and methods, teachers should refer to *STL*, but the statements there should not be used as criteria for rote memorization of factual information and routine procedures. The student who can merely recite the standards is not necessarily progressing toward technological literacy. The student who demonstrates *understanding* and uses the content, concepts, and principles that *STL* describes is becoming technologically literate.

These student assessment standards apply to assessment of student technological literacy in any K–12 classroom.

Definition of Student Assessment

For the purposes of this document, student assessment is defined as the systematic, multi-step process of collecting evidence on student learning, understanding, and abilities and using that information to inform instruction and provide feedback to the learner, thereby enhancing student learning.

Goals and Purposes of Assessing Technological Literacy

Assessment goals define who and when to assess and what type of assessment tool or method to use. The ultimate goal of these assessment standards is to ensure that all students achieve technological literacy.

The three main purposes of assessment include assessment to assist learning, assessment of individual achievement, and assessment to evaluate programs. (NRC, 2001b)

While the data produced by student assessment are used by many people for a variety of purposes, **the primary purpose of assessment should be to improve teaching and learning**. The National Research Council (NRC) supports this purpose in a report entitled, *Knowing What Students Know: The Science and Design of Educational Assessment* (2001b). This report stipulates three main purposes of assessment:

1. Assessment to assist learning
2. Assessment of individual achievement
3. Assessment to evaluate programs

These student assessment standards focus on Purposes 1 and 2. Standards for Purpose 3 are addressed in chapter 4, "Professional Development Standards," and provided in chapter 5, "Program Standards." Therefore, the primary goal of student assessment

should be to collect data on the knowledge and abilities of each individual student and to use this information to improve the teaching and learning process for all students.

The purpose of assessment must be considered when designing assessment tools and methods. For example, teachers may need to collect more or different information to determine if students can *demonstrate* a specific process than they would to determine if students can *explain* the same process. Furthermore, when applying or interpreting assessment data, teachers, administrators, and policymakers should recall the original purpose of the assessment tool or method. Care must be taken to prevent isolated assessment results from becoming representations of the larger educational system.

Table 5. Sample Assessment Approaches for Technological Literacy
Computerized Assessment
Demonstrations/Presentations/Multimedia
Individual and Group Activities
Informal Observations/Discussions
Open-Ended Questioning
Paper-and-Pencil Tests
Peer Assessment
Performances
Portfolios
Projects/Products/Media
Reports/Research
Rubrics/Checklists
Student Interviews – Written and Oral
Student Self Reflection/Assessment
Videos/Slide Shows/Posters
Work Samples

In any case, a singular assessment tool or method is unlikely to achieve all three NRC-identified purposes of assessment: "In general, the more purposes a single assessment aims to serve, the more each purpose will be compromised" (NRC, 2001b, pp. 40–41). Because no single tool or method can "do it all," assessment of technological literacy should utilize multiple approaches to assess both student cognition and performance (see Table 5).

Program Permeability

The vision behind the student assessment standards calls on teachers, administrators, and policymakers to perpetuate interchange between elements of the program, including content, professional development, curricula, instruction, student assessment, and the learning environment, in all areas of learning. The standards and guidelines in chapters 3, 4, and 5 of *AETL* are overlapping in nature to facilitate such interchange.

Audiences for "Student Assessment Standards"

Primary audience:
- Teachers

Other targeted audiences:
- Students
- Parents
- Administrators
- Supervisors
- Teacher Educators
- Policymakers
- General Public

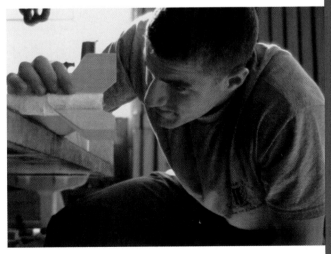

Standard A-1: Assessment of student learning will be consistent with *Standards for Technological Literacy: Content for the Study of Technology (STL)*.

When appropriately used, classroom-based formative assessment positively affects learning. (Black & Wiliam, 1998)

*S*TL articulates what every student should know and be able to do in technology, the content that enables students to use, manage, assess, and understand technology. Assessment may be designed to further the goals of *STL*, serving not only to *assess* but also to *advance* technological literacy. For example, assessment may be designed to present students with situations that are unfamiliar to determine how well students can use what they have learned previously. This requires students to build on prior knowledge, interests, experiences, and abilities and aids them in becoming independent learners. P. Black and D. Wiliam (1998) revealed that when appropriately used, classroom-based formative assessment positively affects learning.

Adherence to standards ensures comprehensiveness in assessing technological literacy, but *STL* does not prescribe an assessment tool or method. Ideas, concepts, and principles that add to *STL* may be included in assessment. Assessment must be flexible and easily modified, reflective of the dynamic, evolving nature of technology.

Correlates with Standard A-2: Student assessment that is consistent with *STL* should be explicitly matched to its intended purpose.

Correlates with Standard A-3: Student assessment that is consistent with *STL* should be derived from research-based assessment principles.

Correlates with Standard A-4: Student assessment that is consistent with *STL* will reflect practical contexts consistent with the nature of technology.

Correlates with Standard PD-1: For student assessment to be consistent with *STL*, teachers must attain knowledge, abilities, and understanding consistent with *STL*.

Correlates with Standard PD-3: For student assessment to be consistent with *STL*, teachers must be prepared to design and evaluate technology curricula and programs.

Correlates with Standard P-1: For student assessment to be consistent with *STL*, technology program development must be consistent with *STL*.

Correlates with Standard P-3: For student assessment to be consistent with *STL*, technology program evaluation must ensure and facilitate technological literacy for all students.

Refer to *STL* Standards 1-20: *STL* identifies the knowledge and abilities students must develop in their progression toward technological literacy in Grades K–12.

NOTE: Additional correlations and references at the guideline level can be found in Appendix E.

Guidelines for meeting Standard A-1 require that teachers consistently

A. Administer comprehensive planning and development across disciplines. Assessment of technological literacy is administered across disciplines. Students study technology in all content areas, as appropriate, to develop technological literacy. Assessment is planned and developed accordingly to determine student progression toward technological literacy.

B. Incorporate comprehensive planning and development across grade levels. Assessment is planned in conjunction with the ongoing nature of the study of technology throughout Grades K–12. Assessment coordinates with the *STL* benchmarks, which are appropriate to specific grade levels (K–2, 3–5, 6–8, and 9–12). Attaining technological literacy is ongoing throughout the student educational experience, and assessment accommodates this goal.

C. Include cognitive learning elements for solving technological problems. Assessment provides all students with opportunities to research and develop, design, invent and innovate, experiment, and troubleshoot. Students are given opportunities to explain, interpret, and apply knowledge.

D. Include psychomotor learning elements for applying technology. Assessment is based on student performance (performance-based assessment),

giving students the opportunity to demonstrate their abilities to use and apply technological knowledge and skills as well as adjust their understandings in novel, diverse, and difficult contexts. Assessment involves gathering data on how well a student is able to do something using tactile (hands-on) knowledge.

E. Guide student abilities to operate within the affective domain, utilizing perspective, empathy, and self assessment. Assessment activities focus on student abilities to grasp the significance of technology in its many forms. Simulations or real applications require students to perform tasks that demonstrate their knowledge and understanding of the positive and negative impacts and consequences in the development and use of technology. Students are assessed on how well they evaluate different points of view and adopt critical perspectives. Students are assessed on their ability to empathize; for example, they might be asked to investigate the processes, procedures, and frustrations of an inventor or innovator of a particular artifact. Students are encouraged to self assess their current abilities as well as their past performance, asking questions such as: How have my activities shown improvement? How might I do this differently if given the opportunity to do it again?

Advancing Excellence in Technological Literacy: Student Assessment, Professional Development, and Program Standards

Standard A-2: Assessment of student learning will be explicitly matched to the intended purpose.

Effective assessment incorporates a variety of formative and summative practices and provides all students with the opportunity to demonstrate their understanding and abilities. Formative assessment is ongoing assessment in the classroom. It provides information to students and teachers to improve teaching and learning. Summative assessment is the cumulative assessment that usually occurs at the end of a unit, topic, project, or problem. It identifies what students have learned and judges student performance against previously identified standards. Summative assessment is most often thought of as final exams, but it also may be a portfolio of student work.

Student assessment usually summons an image of final exams or other large-scale assessment tools and methods. Such assessment does not reflect the full possibilities associated with day-to-day classroom assessment. Teachers must be aware of the useful information assessment provides about student learning during routine activities and interactions. Note, however, that even routine assessment must have clarity of purpose and be explicitly matched to the intended purpose.

Correlates with Standard A-1: Student assessment that is explicitly matched to its intended purpose should be consistent with *STL*.

Correlates with Standard A-3: Student assessment that is explicitly matched to its intended purpose should be derived from research-based assessment principles.

Correlates with Standard PD-3: For student assessment to be explicitly matched to its intended purpose, teachers must be prepared to design and evaluate technology curricula and programs.

Correlates with Standard P-3: For student assessment to be explicitly matched to its intended purpose, technology program evaluation should ensure and facilitate technological literacy for all students.

Refer to *STL* Standards 1-20: *STL* provides the content for the study of technology at the elementary, middle, and high school levels. Accordingly, assessment should have purpose rooted in *STL*.

NOTE: Additional correlations and references at the guideline level can be found in Appendix E.

Guidelines for meeting Standard A-2 require that teachers consistently

A. Formulate a statement of purpose for assessment tools. The purpose of the assessment tool is clear to students as well as other audiences, to ensure accurate interpretation of assessment data. The purpose establishes focus and ensures that the required information is collected. Assessment is an open process, where students are informed about what they need to know, what they should be able to do, how they will demonstrate their knowledge and abilities, and what the impacts of assessment will be. The purpose is coordinated with *STL* to establish a basis for accurate comparison of technological literacy levels against formalized standards.

B. Identify and consider the intended audience in designing assessment tools and reporting assessment data. Teachers consider the intended audience in analyzing and reporting the results of student assessment. If assessment is intended to assist student learning, it may have a very limited audience: the student only or the student and the teacher. If assessment is to determine what level of technological literacy a student has achieved, the intended audience may be broader, including parents, administrators, policymakers, and even the general public.

C. Utilize fair and equitable student assessment methods. Teachers discuss student expectations openly with students prior to learning activities, and student expectations remain consistent throughout the assessment process. Consequently, students are aware of how they must demonstrate their knowledge and abilities. Assessment accommodates student ability levels. Assessment does not attempt to "trick" students. Furthermore, students and teachers recognize there is more than one path to success. Assessment focuses on helping students develop technological literacy rather than having students produce rote responses without any understanding. Assessment methods measure the correctness of the underlying assumptions in a design or technological solution and the appropriateness of the solution in meeting the criteria and constraints. While it is acknowledged that some solutions are, in fact, better than others, care is taken to ensure that incorrect work leading to misunderstanding is corrected.

D. Establish valid and reliable measurements that are reflective of classroom experiences. Teachers utilize valid and reliable assessment tools and methods in which the intended goals of assessment are achieved. Assessment provides a means to produce measurable evidence of learning. Validity and reliability are considered for both formative and summative assessment. Validity is used to help assure that assessment matches the identified purpose. Teachers reflect upon the definitions of validity and reliability and know that validity focuses on the accuracy or truth of the information (data) collected in the assessment process, while reliability attempts to answer concerns about the consistency of the information (data) collected. Careful documentation and systematic observation provide an effective assessment environment. To address reliability and avoid the possibility of bias, assessment data are drawn from several sources.

Advancing Excellence in Technological Literacy: Student Assessment, Professional Development, and Program Standards

Standard A-3: Assessment of student learning will be systematic and derived from research-based assessment principles.

Assessment should be based on the three pillars of the assessment triangle—cognition, observation, and interpretation. (NRC, 2001b)

The National Research Council's *Knowing What Students Know* (NRC, 2001b) discusses the science and design of assessment. It asserts that one type of assessment does not fit all individuals. Assessment is always a process of reasoning from evidence. By its nature, assessment "only estimates . . . what a person knows and can do" (NRC, 2001b, p. 2). Assessment should be based on the three pillars of the assessment triangle—cognition, observation, and interpretation—which must be explicitly connected and designed as a coordinated whole (NRC, 2001b). Like curricula, assessment should be designed to accommodate a variety of developmental levels and intelligences as well as provide pre-assessment activities to familiarize all students with the content.

Research indicates that learning occurs in a holistic fashion and includes knowledge, ways of thinking and acting, and the capability to use knowledge in the real world (NAE & NRC, 2002). Assessment should involve close transfer of prior knowledge and experience and be consistently structured to assess tasks from a well-planned curriculum. "[Assessment should] be aligned with curriculum and instruction if it is to support learning" (NRC, 2001b, p. 3).

"[Assessment should] be aligned with curriculum and instruction if it is to support learning." (NRC, 2001b, p. 3)

Correlates with Standard A-1: Student assessment that is systematic and research-based should be consistent with *STL*.

Correlates with Standard A-2: Student assessment that is systematic and research-based will be explicitly matched to its intended purpose.

Correlates with Standard PD-2: For student assessment to be systematic and research-based, teachers must attain educational perspectives on students as learners of technology.

Correlates with Standard PD-3: For student assessment to be systematic and research-based, teachers must be prepared to design and evaluate technology curricula and programs that enable all students to attain technological literacy.

Correlates with Standard P-3: For student assessment to be systematic and research-based, technology program evaluation must ensure and facilitate technological literacy for all students.

NOTE: Additional correlations and references at the guideline level can be found in Appendix E.

Guidelines for meeting Standard A-3 require that teachers consistently

A. Remain current with research on student learning and assessment.

Teachers consider current research on how students acquire new knowledge, how that new knowledge is connected to past understandings, and how future learning can be enhanced through assessment. Teachers design assessment tools and methods according to current research. For example, formative assessment, or assessment to assist learning, is a primary purpose for performing assessment.

B. Devise a formative assessment plan.

Formative assessment is planned but adaptable, incorporating both formal and informal techniques. For example, appropriate and unobtrusive assessment is used to determine what misconceptions students may be developing. Formative assessment tools and methods could include questioning students, listening to students, and observing students. Formative assessment is interwoven throughout instruction and provides information on the effectiveness

Advancing Excellence in Technological Literacy: Student Assessment, Professional Development, and Program Standards

of instruction. This type of assessment may involve student presentations or demonstrations, either individually or collectively. Formative assessment reveals student progress toward technological literacy. For example, rather than simply revealing that a student does not understand a design process, formative assessment reveals details of the misunderstanding and identifies where the student has missed a key concept. Formative assessment is primarily used to facilitate instructional adjustment in order to enhance student learning.

C. Establish a summative assessment plan. Summative assessment occurs at prescribed intervals and pro-

vides information on the level of student attainment of technological literacy. For example, the most common form of summative assessment is conducted by teachers at the end of a unit of study or at the end of a grading period. Summative assessment tools and methods may include student learning activities that are used to build on previous knowledge, such as student work presented in a portfolio. Formalized assessment allows accurate comparison of assessment results, and technological literacy assessment tools and methods should be based upon the principles in *STL*.

D. Facilitate enhancement of student learning.

Assessment is relevant to students and to the learning goal. Assessment promotes learning by providing an opportunity for students to apply knowledge and abilities while offering feedback related to their understandings. Assessment is a continuous process, an integral part of instruction and the larger classroom and educational experiences. Accordingly, students reflect upon assessment results to modify their learning, and teachers reflect upon assessment results to adjust instruction.

E. Accommodate for student commonality and diversity.

Assessment is designed with consideration for students. Recognition is given to student similarities and differences, including interests, cultures, abilities, socio-economic backgrounds, and special needs. Teachers acknowledge that accommodating students may require multiple instruments to assess a single idea or concept. Unexpected responses are considered in light of prior student experiences, which influence student reactions to unique situations. For example, assessment may sometimes provide teachers and students with results that are the consequence of misconceptions that students have developed over time. Teachers are prepared for this and adjust instruction and future lessons and assessment tools and methods accordingly.

F. Include students in the assessment process.

Students are involved in the assessment process, making them aware of what is expected of them. Students are provided with opportunities to learn more about the assessment process and even participate in establishing the criteria, such as in establishing criteria for an assessment rubric. Students are given opportunities for self and peer assessment, requiring them to expand on their own critical thinking. Students may be provided with options to work in teams, pairs, or individually, which impacts the assessment process.

Advancing Excellence in Technological Literacy: Student Assessment, Professional Development, and Program Standards

Advancing Excellence in Technological Literacy: Student Assessment, Professional Development, and Program Standards

Description

This formative assessment uses questioning as a method for obtaining student feedback. The student feedback is then used to inform instruction, thereby increasing instructional effectiveness. This vignette illustrates *AETL* Standard A-3 B, D, and F.

Adapted from a vignette written by Anna Sumner.

Formative Assessment:

Using Student Feedback

Assessment Purpose

The purpose of this formative assessment is to assist student learning by assessing student understanding of the historical influence of technology.

Audience for Assessment Data

As this assessment is intended to enhance student learning and ensure effective instruction, the data collected will only be available to the student and to the teacher.

STL Standards Assessed

- Standard 4, Benchmarks D, E, F, G
- Standard 6, Benchmarks D, F, G

Grade Level Appropriateness

Grade 7

Note: While this vignette highlights a seventh grade classroom, questioning techniques may be applied in classrooms at any grade level for formative assessment.

A social studies lesson was designed to further student understanding of technology and its implications on society from a historical perspective. Students understood technology as "the innovation, change, or modification of the natural environment to satisfy perceived human needs and wants" (ITEA, 2000a, p. 242) but had not previously considered technology's historical influence on society. A lesson was developed to engage students in a discussion on the societal implications of technology throughout history.

Ms. Yu initiated the lesson by asking questions to determine what students believed were the influences of technology on history. The questions were developed prior to the lesson and included: *How has history been influenced by technology? What can be learned from the past regarding the development of new technologies? How has the development of new technologies historically influenced society? What is uncertain about the development of new technologies in relation to society?* Students were informed of their roles in the process, and their responses were documented to provide an opportunity for Ms. Yu to review and evaluate the feedback. Questioning revealed student thinking, including understandings and misunderstandings. As the lesson proceeded, student responses provided direction for the remainder of the lesson and instruction.

Ms. Yu continued to judge student learning by identifying additional questions that made student thinking visible. Ms. Yu questioned students, listened to students, and observed students. As the lesson progressed, she asked questions about the management of technology and included: *How* can society deal with the continuously changing nature of technology? Can society "manage" technology to prevent new developments from causing it to feel out of control? How can technology be managed to provide the most benefit and least amount of harm?

At the conclusion of the lesson, feedback was again gathered to assess student understanding. Students were asked, *How can societal values and beliefs be protected in a world that is increasingly technologically dependent?* As students provided responses, Ms. Yu was able to compare the ideas shared with those shared throughout the progression of the lesson. Ms. Yu was able to determine which concepts future lessons should focus on to enhance student understandings while dispelling misunderstandings.

Additionally, Ms. Yu asked the students questions related to the format of instruction rather than the content of the lesson. Student responses could be used to revise the lesson format and enhance future instruction. Such questions included: *What did you like/dislike about this lesson? Why? Be specific! What did you learn about the societal implications of technology? What additional information would have been helpful for your understanding of the societal implications of technology?* Generalities such as: "Because it was fun" or "It was boring" were not accepted. Students were required to validate their opinions. Questioning ended with: *What could be done to improve this lesson/activity? Be specific!* Once again, students were required to validate their opinions.

Ms. Yu set aside reflective time to assess gathered feedback and make judgements regarding the quality of her instruction. Ms. Yu revised the activities and curricula to correct student misconceptions and enhance student learning.

Ms. Yu retained the information obtained through feedback to use later, when she reassessed program revisions. She knew that a chronological record would be useful in judging program progression throughout the implementation process.

A-4 | Practical Contexts

Standard A-4: Assessment of student learning will reflect practical contexts consistent with the nature of technology.

"Research on learning finds that many students learn best in experiential ways—by doing, rather than only seeing or hearing—and the study of technology emphasizes and capitalizes on such active learning." (ITEA, 2000a, p. 5)

"Research on learning finds that many students learn best in experiential ways—by doing, rather than only seeing or hearing—and the study of technology emphasizes and capitalizes on such active learning" (ITEA, 2000a, p. 5). Likewise, student assessment must reflect the active, dynamic nature of the study of technology and the manner in which people draw upon and exercise knowledge and abilities acquired through experience. The practical contexts, which are consistent with the essence of technology, are found in *STL*. Assessment should draw from a variety of sources and involve a mixture of opportunities for students to demonstrate their understanding, abilities, and critical-thinking skills.

Teachers should use a variety of assessment tools and methods that require students to use higher-order thinking skills. For example, holistic approaches to assessment take forms other than traditional paper-and-pencil tests and can measure abilities that traditional tests cannot. Holistic approaches may include demonstrated performance and student portfolios as a natural course of instruction and authentic assessment that requires students to perform complex tasks representative of real life.

Correlates with Standard A-1: Student assessment that reflects practical contexts consistent with the nature of technology should be consistent with *STL*.

Correlates with Standard PD-1: For student assessment to reflect practical contexts consistent with the nature of technology, teachers must attain knowledge, abilities, and understanding consistent with *STL*.

Correlates with Standard PD-3: For student assessment to reflect practical contexts consistent with the nature of technology, teachers must be prepared to design and evaluate technology curricula and programs that enable all students to attain technological literacy.

Correlates with Standard P-1: For student assessment to reflect practical contexts consistent with the nature of technology, technology program development must be consistent with *STL*.

Correlates with Standard P-3: For student assessment to reflect practical contexts consistent with the nature of technology, technology program evaluation must ensure and facilitate technological literacy for all students.

Refer to *STL* Standards 1-20: *STL* identifies the knowledge and abilities students must develop in their progression toward technological literacy in Grades K–12.

NOTE: Additional correlations and references at the guideline level can be found in Appendix E.

Guidelines for meeting Standard A-4 require that teachers consistently

A. Incorporate technological problem solving. Assessment provides teachers with feedback about what students actually know and can do. Assessment may require students to identify technological problems, needs, and opportunities within a cultural context; write and construct problem statements; design, develop, model, test, prototype, and implement solutions; analyze, evaluate, refine, and redesign solutions; and reflect and assign value to processes and outcomes. For example, students working in groups over a period of days or weeks might examine a local technological issue and develop recommendations for correcting a potential problem. Students make mistakes and learn that mistakes can lead to successes.

B. Include variety in technological content and performance-based methods. Assessment models laboratory-classroom experiences. Assessment incorporates multiple *STL* standards to highlight the interrelationships among technologies and the connections between technology and other disciplines. Assessment uses new contexts to allow students to make connections with other technologies. Consequently, students realize that technology is not simply a group of artifacts but involves a specialized method of thinking and solving problems across a range of contexts or disciplines. Multiple methods of performance assessment provide information that is readily accessible and easy to read and understand, allowing teachers to gather diverse information about student progress toward technological literacy. Therefore, each assessment method

may provide different information about student understanding of content.

C. Facilitate critical thinking and decision making. Assessment requires measuring critical thinking and transfer of knowledge to new situations. Teachers may use a pre- and post-test approach to determine how students have grown in their understanding and abilities as a direct result of instruction. Students may

> Teachers help students understand where they are and should be in their development of technological literacy.

write about their understanding in reflective responses to questions, or they may be directed to write to someone, such as a younger student who has not experienced the topic, to explain their understanding of it. Students may be required to respond to a problem situation to demonstrate their critical-thinking and decision-making skills. Teachers help students understand where they are and

Advancing Excellence in Technological Literacy: Student Assessment, Professional Development, and Program Standards

should be in their development of technological literacy.

D. Accommodate for modification to student assessment.
Assessment of technological literacy is flexible and easily modified, reflective of the dynamic, evolving nature of technology. For example, assessment enables modifications to accommodate new advances in technology, current trends in technological products, and research on student learning and assessment.

E. Utilize authentic assessment.
Students are required to perform complex tasks using what they have learned and appropriate technological resources. For example, students are assessed on their abilities to make accurate measurements; to use appropriate technology, science, and mathematics principles; to be creative in designing technological solutions; and also on the rigor of their methodology and the quality of the questions they pursue. Students are required to demonstrate their knowledge and abilities by creating a response or product that resembles practical experiences. Many different levels of literacy are assessed in contexts that closely mirror situations that students experience in real life as well as the context in which the abilities were learned.

Summative Assessment:

Student Product Development Portfolio

Assessment Purpose

The purpose of this summative assessment is to identify cumulative student understanding and abilities related to design and the design process based on a collection of student work presented in a portfolio.

Audience for Assessment Data

As this assessment is summative, the data collected will be available to students, parents, and the teacher.

STL Standards Assessed

- Standard 8, Benchmarks H, I, J, K
- Standard 11, Benchmarks M, N, O, P, Q, R

Grade Level Appropriateness

Grades 9–12

Note: While this vignette highlights a high school laboratory-classroom, student portfolios may be used at any grade level for summative assessment.

Students in Mr. Morales' technology class were grouped in teams and instructed to design and construct a product, either by improving an existing product or developing a new one. Prior to the initiation of this assessment, students were instructed on the concepts of design, product development, entrepreneurship, and the designed world. A rubric was provided (see pp. 34–35) to allow students to monitor their own progress consistent with the criteria that would be used to assess final solutions. Students were given the following sequential instructions:

1. **Develop a Group Proposal.** Brainstorm to identify the product. Determine the product's design parameters (such as function/purpose, size, cost, and eventual disposal). Identify features of the product, staying within the design parameters. The group proposal should include sketches and/or drawings and a formal market survey that identifies market need. It may also include advertisements.

2. **Develop a Prototype of the New or Refined Product.** Design plans and procedures for construction or improvements of the product. Follow proper construction techniques to produce a prototype of the product. For example, write plans using appropriate design symbols, follow safety guidelines, demonstrate safe use of equipment, and demonstrate the ability to create technical instructions.

(instructions continued on p. 35)

Description

This summative assessment provides information on the level of technological literacy attained by students. Using student portfolios, students were given the option to either improve an existing product or to design and develop a new product to meet a human want or need. This assignment could be adapted to a variety of laboratory-classroom settings. This vignette illustrates *AETL* Standard A-3 C and Standard A-4 B, C, and E.

Adapted from a vignette written by Mike Lindstrom and Joe Nelson.

Advancing Excellence in Technological Literacy: Student Assessment, Professional Development, and Program Standards

Sample Feedback Rubrics for Assessing Student Products and Portfolios

	Assessment of Student Product			
	Unsatisfactory (1 Point)	Satisfactory (2 Points)	Above Average (3 Points)	Excellent (4 Points)
Identification of product	• Product and design parameters identified.	• Product and design parameters identified. • Market research establishes need.	• Product and design parameters identified. • Market research establishes need. • Evidence of research and investigation.	• Product and design parameters identified. • Market research establishes need. • Evidence of research and investigation. • Minimum of 10 design ideas brainstormed.
Identification of criteria and constraints	• Design proposed. • No indication of a development plan.	• Development or production plan outlined.	• Development or production plan outlined. • Evidence to indicate consideration of resources.	• Development or production plan outlined. • Evidence to indicate consideration of resources. • Trade-offs defined. • Jigs and/or fixtures proposed.
Use of prototyping/ modeling	• Observed laboratory safety.	• Observed laboratory safety. • Prototype or model developed.	• Observed laboratory safety. • Prototype or model developed. • Alternatives considered but not reflected in model.	• Observed laboratory safety. • Prototype or model appropriate. • Multiple design iterations modeled. • Reflection of criteria and constraints apparent.
Evaluation of design	• Evaluation of product. • No indication of consideration of market need.	• Evaluation of product. • Market need reflected in evaluation.	• Evaluation of product. • Market need reflected in evaluation. • Design solution evaluated against criteria and constraints.	• Evaluation of product includes critique of the design process and the final product. • Market need reflected in evaluation. • Design solution evaluated against criteria and constraints. • Future design recommendations proposed.
Prototype of Product	• Aesthetically pleasing.	• Aesthetically pleasing. • Demonstrates creativity.	• Aesthetically pleasing. • Demonstrates creativity. • Quality workmanship.	• Aesthetically pleasing. • Demonstrates creativity. • Quality workmanship. • Satisfies market need.

Assessment of Student Portfolio				
	Unsatisfactory (1 Point)	Satisfactory (2 Points)	Above Average (3 Points)	Excellent (4 Points)
Organization	• No sequence to presentation.	• Only beginning and end stages of product design detailed.	• Entire design process detailed. • Market research and concept creation not presented.	• Entire design process, market research, and concept creation detailed.
Content Relevancy	• Graphics and/or illustrations highlight final product. • No reflection of the development process.	• Graphics and/or illustrations highlight final product. • Little reflection of the development process.	• Graphics and/or illustrations highlight product development process. • Narratives highlight product development process. • Reflection questions addressed.	• Graphics and/or illustrations highlight product development process. • Narratives highlight product development process. • Reflection questions addressed. • Narratives highlight environmental analysis. • Multiple examples (5+) provided.
Presentation	• No narrative provided to highlight design process.	• Minimal narrative provided. • Minimum of 4 graphics and/or illustrations.	• Narratives indicate student reflection. • Minimum of 7 graphics and/or illustrations.	• Narratives indicate student reflection. • Minimum of 10 graphics and/or illustrations. • Captions detail illustrations. • Aesthetically pleasing.

3. **Evaluate the Prototype.** Upon completing construction of the prototype, conduct an environmental analysis of the material list, stating the impact and life of the product, recyclability of the materials, and expected future impacts of the product's use. Then answer the following:

   a. Does the product meet the design specifications?
   b. Does the product fit the need of the market?
   c. Do the instructions and plans provide complete information for assembly of the product or modification of the existing product?
   d. Does the quality of the product meet or exceed market expectations?

Rubrics guided both students and the teacher in consistently assessing student work. The rubrics defined the assessment characteristics and quality of work demanded by the final product and portfolio. The rubrics used a scale of 1–4, with the highest quality work represented by a 4 and the lowest quality acceptable work represented by a 1. Students who did not meet minimum expectations in a given category received no credit for that category.

Standard A-5: Assessment of student learning will incorporate data collection for accountability, professional development, and program enhancement.

"Something important should be learned from every assessment situation, and the information gained should ultimately help improve learning." (NRC, 2001b, p. 8)

"Something important should be learned from every assessment situation, and the information gained should ultimately help improve learning" (NRC, 2001b, p. 8). Classroom and large-scale assessment tools and methods must be designed with the end use in mind. Large-scale assessment tools and methods are, by nature, not conducive to providing immediate feedback to students and teachers. To make them immediately useful for teachers and students, they should incorporate active learning techniques, such as meta-cognition (thinking about thinking), allowing large-scale assessment tools and methods to "provide positive direction for instruction" (NRC, 2001b, p. 8). Assessment involves the process of collecting data, interpreting the results, and reporting the results. The results can then be used to make decisions that directly affect the understanding and development of technological literacy.

It must be acknowledged that assessment can be designed to provide data that are relevant beyond the classroom. When assessment is based on *STL*, the data obtained enable technological literacy comparisons within classrooms, schools, school districts, and states/provinces/regions as well as across nations. The increasing demand for a technologically literate populace will impact decisions on effectively incorporating the study of technology into the educational system. Accurate assessment data can help guide this process.

Correlates with Standards A-1–A-4: Student assessment that incorporates data collection for accountability, professional development, and program enhancement should be consistent with Standards A-1, A-2, A-3, and A-4.

Correlates with Standard PD-3: For student assessment to incorporate data collection for accountability, professional development, and program enhancement, teachers must be prepared to design and evaluate curricula and programs that enable all students to attain technological literacy.

Correlates with Standard PD-7: Student assessment data should be used by professional development providers who plan, implement, and evaluate the pre-service and in-service education of teachers.

Correlates with Standards P-1–P-5: Student assessment data should be used in conjunction with Standards P-1, P-2, P-3, P-4, and P-5 to guide program enhancement decisions.

NOTE: Additional correlations and references at the guideline level can be found in Appendix E.

Guidelines for meeting Standard A-5 require that teachers consistently

A. Maintain data collection for accountability. Assessment acknowledges the rights of students, parents, and other interested parties to know how well students are performing. Assessment data provide information about student ideas and misconceptions, not just a listing of grades from quizzes and tests. That is, assessment data reflect student learning, which permits the data to be used moment-by-moment in the laboratory-classroom, affecting instructional decisions. Similarly, assessment data are used in short-range planning to adjust instruction to the needs of students. Long-range planning uses assessment data to ensure that every student learns important technological material to enhance the development of technological literacy.

B. Use student assessment results to help guide professional development decisions. Student assessment results are used to indicate areas in which professional development is needed. The need for both pre-service and in-service of teachers to align course content, curricula, instruction, and student assessment is discussed in more detail in chapter 4, "Professional Development Standards."

C. Use student assessment results to help guide program enhancement decisions. Just as programs, curricula, and instruction impact assessment in a top-down implementation approach, assessment impacts instruction, curricula, and programs in a bottom-up, systemic fashion, inspiring revision and refinement as appropriate. The need for program coherency is discussed in more detail in chapter 5, "Program Standards."

Advancing Excellence in Technological Literacy: Student Assessment, Professional Development, and Program Standards

Professional Development Standards

The standards in this chapter are intended for use by professional development providers and by local, district, state/provincial/regional, and national/federal entities to ensure effective and continuous pre-service and in-service education for technology teachers and other content area teachers. These professional development standards are aligned with *Standards for Technological Literacy: Content for the Study of Technology (STL)* (ITEA, 2000a). They are developed to be implemented in conjunction with *STL* as well as with the student assessment and program standards included in *Advancing Excellence in Technological Literacy: Student Assessment, Professional Development, and Program Standards (AETL)*. Therefore, these standards are of optimal use when curricula and instruction used in professional development have incorporated the concepts and principles identified in *STL*.

These professional development standards are based on input from professional development providers, including teacher educators, supervisors, and administrators. The standards also reflect attributes of effective professional development such as those described in *Designing Professional Development for Teachers of Science and Mathematics* (Loucks-Horsley, Hewson, Love, & Stiles, 1998):

> Effective professional development experiences foster collegiality and collaboration; promote experimentation and risk taking; draw their content from available knowledge bases; involve participants in decisions about as many aspects of the professional development experience as possible; provide time to participate, reflect on, and practice what is learned; provide leadership and sustained support; supply appropriate rewards and incentives; have designs that reflect knowledge bases on learning and change; integrate individual, school, and district goals; and integrate both organizationally and instructionally with other staff development and change efforts. (p. 36)

Research indicates that "professional development [should] help teachers understand (a) subject matter, (b) learners and learning, and (c) teaching methods" (Loucks-Horsley & Matsumoto, 1999, p. 262). In addition to acquiring a knowledge base related to teaching and learning technology, teachers should be taught in ways reflective of how they are being asked to teach (Sparks, 1997). Accordingly, Standards 1–6 outline the content of professional development, and Standard 7 addresses the process of professional development.

These standards apply to the professional development of every teacher who educates students about technology, not only technology teachers who operate primarily within the technology laboratory-classroom and whose major responsibility is delivering technology instruction. For example, these standards are eminently suitable for a social studies teacher who is teaching the social influence of technology or the history of technology. The ultimate goal is for all students to achieve technological literacy.

Definition of Professional Development

For the purposes of this document, professional development is defined as a continuous process of lifelong learning and growth that begins early in life, continues through the undergraduate, pre-service experience, and extends through the in-service years.

> **Note:** For the purposes of the professional development standards, the term *teacher* refers to both pre-service and in-service teachers, unless otherwise indicated.

The Continuous Nature of Professional Development

Professional development of teachers is an ongoing process in which teachers acquire increasingly comprehensive levels of content knowledge, pedagogical skills, and knowledge of how students learn. This is consistent with the dynamic, evolving nature of technology. The standards for professional development should be considered target outcomes of the professional development continuum. These standards describe the knowledge and abilities that teachers should acquire as the result of engaging in professional development.

Technology teachers take various pathways to get to the classroom, including college- or university-based teacher preparation programs and a variety of alternate routes. Thus, it is not practical to specify when and how these target outcomes will be met or achieved. Teachers who have completed a traditional

technology teacher preparation program should attain all of these standards at a basic level. Teachers of other content areas receiving instruction in disciplines other than technology may be more reliant upon in-service opportunities to attain the professional development standards. Through continued professional development, technology teachers and other content area teachers should achieve greater breadth and depth of knowledge and competence related to technology over time.

Program Permeability

The vision behind the professional development standards calls on teachers, administrators, and policymakers to perpetuate interchange between elements of the program, including content, professional development, curricula, instruction, student assessment, and the learning environment, in all areas of learning. The standards and guidelines in chapters 3, 4, and 5 of *AETL* are overlapping in nature to facilitate such interchange.

Audiences for "Professional Development Standards"

Primary audience:

- Professional Development Providers (including Teacher Educators, Supervisors, and Administrators)

Other targeted audiences:

- Teachers
- Policymakers
- Association Leaders
- General Public

Standard PD-1: Professional development will provide teachers with knowledge, abilities, and understanding consistent with *Standards for Technological Literacy: Content for the Study of Technology (STL)*.

For teachers to be able to educate students about technology, they must be technologically literate themselves. Therefore, technology teachers and other content area teachers need to develop knowledge and abilities consistent with *STL* so they can help students achieve technological literacy. Teachers must:

1. Know the implications of technology as the modification of the natural environment to satisfy perceived human needs and wants.
2. Understand the nature of technology, the impact of technology on society, and the basic concepts of design.
3. Be able to "do" technology, acquiring essential abilities for our technological world.
4. Develop an awareness of the designed world in which we live.

Specific technologies are influenced by a variety of factors, including the needs of individuals, groups, and society as a whole; however, certain core concepts permeate all technologies. These include systems, resources, requirements (criteria and constraints), optimization and trade-offs, processes, and controls.

Correlates with Standard PD-2: Knowledge, abilities, and understanding consistent with *STL* are necessary for teachers to have educational perspectives on students as learners of technology.

Correlates with Standard PD-3: Knowledge, abilities, and understanding consistent with *STL* are necessary for teachers to design and evaluate technology curricula and programs.

Correlates with Standard PD-4: Knowledge, abilities, and understanding consistent with *STL* are necessary for teachers to use instructional strategies that enhance technology teaching, student learning, and student assessment.

Correlates with Standard PD-5: Knowledge, abilities, and understanding consistent with *STL* are necessary for teachers to design and manage learning environments that promote technological literacy.

Correlates with Standard A-1: Teachers provided with knowledge, abilities, and understanding consistent with *STL* will be able to assess student learning consistent with *STL*.

Correlates with Standard A-4: Teachers provided with knowledge, abilities, and understanding consistent with *STL* will be able to assess student learning in a manner that reflects the practical contexts of technology, consistent with its nature.

Correlates with Standard P-1: Teachers provided with knowledge, abilities, and understanding consistent with *STL* will be able to develop technology programs consistent with *STL*.

Refer to *STL* Standards 1-20: For teachers to facilitate student development of technological literacy, they must be technologically literate themselves in accordance with the standards in *STL*.

NOTE: Additional correlations and references at the guideline level can be found in Appendix E.

Guidelines for meeting Standard PD-1 require that professional development providers consistently prepare teachers to

A. Understand the nature of technology. Professional development incorporates views about the nature of technology, commensurate with Standards 1–3 of *STL*. Teachers learn what technology is (i.e., both tangible and intangible aspects) and how technology is important to daily life. Teachers learn the characteristics, scope, and core concepts of technology and understand how they permeate all technologies. Teachers comprehend the integrative nature that links technology with science, mathematics, engineering, and other disciplines.

B. Recognize the relationship between technology and society. Professional development exhibits the relationship between technology and

society, commensurate with Standards 4–7 of *STL*. Teachers are able to explain that while technology impacts society, society has a major influence on technology, and both technology and society affect the environment. Teachers realize how technology can both create and solve problems. Teachers become aware of the major "eras" of technology, along with specific events and milestones that helped develop the technological world in which we live, and can articulate the influence of technology on history.

C. Know the attributes of design. Professional development incorporates problem solving through design, commensurate with Standards 8–10 of *STL*. Teachers are acquainted with engineering design and other types of problem

solving, such as troubleshooting, research and development, invention and innovation, and experimentation.

D. Develop abilities for a technological world.
Professional development reveals abilities for a technological world, commensurate with Standards 11–13 of *STL*. Teachers gain knowledge and abilities related to the attributes of design, engineering, and other problem-solving techniques and are able to apply their abilities in the laboratory-classroom through a hands-on approach to technology. Teachers develop abilities to use and maintain technological products and systems outside the laboratory-classroom, in everyday life. Teachers are able to evaluate the impact of technological products and systems on individuals, the environment, and society. The design process is

internalized by teachers, providing guidance for activities inside and outside the laboratory-classroom.

E. Develop proficiency in the designed world.
Professional development encourages the utilization of design principles, employment of evaluation methods, interpretation of research, use of modeling techniques, and incorporation of practices related to the designed world, commensurate with Standards 14–20 of *STL*. Teachers investigate the ways our designed world utilizes resources, materials, tools, machines, people, information, energy, capital, and time in the development of products and systems. Teachers recognize the need to remain current with the changing roles of technology and develop abilities to select, use, and maintain the technologies included in the designed world.

Standard PD-2: Professional development will provide teachers with educational perspectives on students as learners of technology.

To effectively guide student learning, teachers must develop an understanding of students and how they learn. Professional development providers should educate teachers to work with all students, regardless of abilities, interests, age levels, or backgrounds. Teachers must work harmoniously with all students to establish valuable bonds and motivate student interest in the study of technology and for learning in general. Teachers should be aware of student learning styles and recognize the importance of providing varied learning opportunities to accommodate students as learners. For example, while some students will understand material presented in a visual manner, teachers need to acknowledge that other students are auditory learners and will process verbal information more effectively. Teachers must be aware of the significance of utilizing cognitive, psychomotor, and affective elements to develop technological literacy and support student understanding.

Correlates with Standard PD-1: Educational perspectives on students as learners of technology require teachers to have knowledge, abilities, and understanding consistent with *STL*.

Correlates with Standard PD-3: Educational perspectives on students as learners of technology are necessary for teachers to design and evaluate technology curricula and programs.

Correlates with Standard PD-4: Educational perspectives on students as learners of technology are necessary for teachers to use instructional strategies that enhance technology teaching, student learning, and student assessment.

Correlates with Standard PD-5 Educational perspectives on students as learners of technology are necessary for teachers to design and manage learning environments that promote technological literacy.

Correlates with Standard A-3: Teachers provided with educational perspectives on students as learners of technology will be able to assess student learning in a manner that is systematic and derived from research-based assessment principles.

Correlates with Standard P-2: Teachers provided with educational perspectives on students as learners of technology will be able to implement technology programs that facilitate technological literacy for all students.

Correlates with Standard P-4: Teachers provided with educational perspectives on students as learners of technology will be able to create and manage learning environments that facilitate technological literacy for all students.

NOTE: Additional correlations and references at the guideline level can be found in Appendix E.

Advancing Excellence in Technological Literacy: Student Assessment, Professional Development, and Program Standards

Guidelines for meeting Standard PD-2 require that professional development providers consistently prepare teachers to

A. Incorporate student commonality and diversity to enrich learning. Through professional development, teachers learn the meaning of developing the technological literacy of all students and also understand how that goal is achieved. Teachers recognize student similarities and differences, including interests, cultures, abilities, socio-economic backgrounds, and special needs. Teachers recognize that diversity can enrich the classroom and are prepared to positively incorporate individual experiences into the learning environment. Teachers learn that students often have preconceptions about the technological world and are educated to identify and correct misconceptions as appropriate.

B. Provide cognitive, psychomotor, and affective learning opportunities. Teachers are prepared, through professional development, to provide students with opportunities to gain and demonstrate knowledge and abilities related to technology that integrate understanding (i.e., knowing + doing = understanding). Teachers learn how to integrate perspective, empathy, student self assessment, and student peer assessment with technological activities. Teachers recognize that simulations or real applications require students to demonstrate their knowledge and understanding. Teachers are pre-

pared to incorporate varied technological activities, representative of practical experiences, requiring students to think critically and make decisions.

C. Assist students in becoming effective learners. Professional development emphasizes the need to establish and maintain productive student-teacher relationships to assist students in becoming effective learners. Teachers develop strategies to support and encourage student learning. Teachers gain abilities to develop learning activities that appeal to student interests and challenge students to reflect on practical experiences. Teachers develop strategies that require students to transfer learning to different situations that promote student creativity and imagination.

D. Conduct and use research on how students learn technology. Through professional development, teachers become aware of current research on students as learners. They understand the difference between learning from a cognitive-based perspective and learning from a psychomotor-based perspective in attaining technological literacy. Teachers understand the need for additional research on students as learners of technology and acquire abilities necessary to conduct educational research.

Standard PD-3: Professional development will prepare teachers to design and evaluate technology curricula and programs.

In many cases, teachers assume responsibility for fashioning content into the overall plan for instruction. The study of technology is relatively new to education, and all teachers should be educated in the process of interpreting *STL* and translating it into curricula and programs. A curriculum delineates content for the classroom. It structures, organizes, balances, and presents the content to the students. The curriculum provides plans for instruction through objectives, activities, lessons, units, courses of study, and student assessment methods. Lesson plans give the teacher a daily operational structure in which to deliver content to students.

STL encompasses a broad scope of technology that cuts across artificial barriers of categorization between technology and other school subjects, such as science, mathematics, social studies, language arts, and other content areas. Teachers should be familiar with

> The study of technology is relatively new to education, and all teachers should be educated in the process of interpreting *STL* and translating it into curricula and programs.

Correlates with Standard PD-1: To design and evaluate technology curricula and programs, teachers must have knowledge, abilities, and understanding consistent with *STL*.

Correlates with Standard PD-2: To design and evaluate technology curricula and programs, teachers must have educational perspectives on students as learners of technology.

Correlates with Standard A-1: Teachers prepared to design and evaluate technology curricula and programs will be able to assess student learning consistent with *STL*.

Correlates with Standard A-2: Teachers prepared to design and evaluate technology curricula and programs will be able to match assessment to the intended purpose.

Correlates with Standard A-3: Teachers prepared to design and evaluate technology curricula and programs will be able to assess student learning in a manner that is systematic and derived from research-based assessment principles.

Correlates with Standard A-4: Teachers prepared to design and evaluate technology curricula and programs will be able to assess student learning in a manner that reflects practical contexts consistent with the nature of technology.

Correlates with Standard A-5: Teachers prepared to design and evaluate technology curricula and programs will be able to incorporate data collection for accountability, professional development, and program enhancement.

Correlates with Standard P-1: Teachers prepared to design and evaluate technology curricula and programs will be able to develop technology programs consistent with *STL*.

Correlates with Standard P-2: Teachers prepared to design and evaluate technology curricula and programs will be able to implement technology programs that facilitate technological literacy for all students.

Correlates with Standard P-3: Teachers prepared to design and evaluate technology curricula and programs will be able to evaluate technology programs to ensure and facilitate technological literacy for all students.

Correlates with Standard P-4: Teachers prepared to design and evaluate technology curricula and programs will be able to create and manage learning environments that facilitate technological literacy for all students.

Correlates with Standard P-5: Teachers prepared to design and evaluate technology curricula and programs will be able to provide management of technology programs.

Refer to *STL* Standards 1–20: Teachers should design and evaluate technology curricula and programs based on the content in *STL*.

NOTE: Additional correlations and references at the guideline level can be found in Appendix E.

---

the content of *STL* and possess the abilities to develop curricula and programs that allow students to study technology. The standards in *STL* are clarified and exemplified by benchmarks appropriate to specific grade levels (K–2, 3–5, 6–8, and 9–12). Reference is made in *STL* to the ongoing nature of technological literacy development beyond Grade 12, both in formal and informal settings. Attaining technological literacy must be ongoing throughout the student educational experience. Teachers should be prepared to develop curricula and programs that facilitate the integrated vision of *STL*.

Teachers should be educated to implement programs in a manner that is consistent with *STL*. Implementation of program curricula incorporates content, instruction, and student assessment. Evaluation of programs should be ongoing and reflect the content in *STL* and *AETL*. Technology teachers and other content area teachers should be prepared to evaluate programs and modify them as necessary to ensure that all students attain technological literacy.

Guidelines for meeting Standard PD-3 require that professional development providers consistently prepare teachers to

A. Design and evaluate curricula and programs that enable all students to attain technological literacy.

As a result of professional development, teachers learn to develop curricula and programs that enable students to learn from multiple (knowing and doing) perspectives. Teachers are prepared in the use of the latest standards-based curriculum development methods. Professional development providers require teachers to be familiar with "Program Standards" (chapter 5) of *AETL*. Teachers recognize curricula and program evaluation as essential and develop strategies to conduct evaluations on a systematic basis. Pre-service and in-service education prepares teachers to develop and implement student assessment and use the results to influence curricula (see chapter 3).

B. Design and evaluate curricula and programs across disciplines.

Professional development prepares teachers to fashion and evaluate curricula and programs that are interdisciplinary. In creating curricula, teachers adapt technology content to integrate it with other disciplines. For example, themes or units of study in space colonization, the industrial revolution, or technological influences on the Civil War provide a rich blend of learning for students in the study of technology. Teachers learn strategies for conducting evaluations across content areas when assessing technological literacy.

C. Design and evaluate curricula and programs across grade levels.

Professional development prepares teachers to fashion and evaluate curricula and programs that provide a continuity of learning from Grades K–12 with connections to life beyond high school. In creating curricula, teachers develop abilities to integrate technology content with technological study at the elementary, middle, and high school levels, promoting interest and motivation to all students, regardless of their experiences. Teachers learn to evaluate curricula and programs across grade levels.

D. Design and evaluate curricula and programs using multiple sources of information. Professional development includes generating and evaluating curricula and programs based upon multiple sources of information and research. Teachers learn to draw upon resources in *STL* as well as other sources dealing with technology. Teachers recognize student assessment results as a source for informing decisions about curricula. Teachers become knowledgeable about standards in other school subjects, including science, mathematics, social studies, language arts, and other content areas. Teachers learn collaborative strategies for working with other teachers across disciplines, providing a rich resource for developing and evaluating curricula. Teachers are prepared to obtain input from stakeholders within the community and school to assist in developing curricula and programs, including other teachers within the department, other teachers within the school, administrators, school leaders, professional development providers, business and industry leaders, engineers, technologists, scientists, and others.

Modeling Professional Practice

Teacher candidates in a *Teaching Transportation Technology* class at a local university were divided into groups. Each group represented a company that designed and sold a particular transportation product. For example, one group received the following information:

> You are members of the R&D team at XYZ Corporation, a company that builds motorized scooters. The market for your product recently expanded due to new innovations developed by your competitors. Unfortunately, your company was in such a rush to capture part of the expanded market that it developed and sold a new scooter model without going through the usual R&D phase of the development cycle. It now appears that this was a mistake. The company has received thousands of complaints, and the product has a number of flaws involving safety, durability, and convenience. You must identify the design flaws and come up with a plan to fix them.

Teacher candidates were provided with specifications for the product (size, weight, etc.). Teacher candidates were instructed to keep a journal, as the activity would be assessed based on the design and problem-solving process evidenced by journal entries. Each group was provided with time to research its product and record individual findings in journals. The groups were then given the following instructions:

Step 1. Draw a picture of the product in your individual journal.

Step 2. As a group, choose one picture to represent the product.

Step 3. Identify the innovations to the product that make it new and exciting, while ensuring its safety, durability, and convenience.

Step 4. As a group, identify at least three definite design flaws, and come up with a checklist of additional items you need to research to ensure that your company is marketing a quality product.

Step 5. Present your product to the class. The class will identify the product's design flaws. These will form the basis for your "consumer complaints."

Description

This professional development activity develops teacher knowledge and abilities to interpret *STL* and translate its content into curricula by modeling teaching practices that technology teachers are expected to use in their laboratory-classrooms. Teacher candidates were instructed to engage in a group research and development activity, using individual journals to record their progress. At the end of the activity, teacher candidates discussed the application of the activity to their future laboratory-classrooms. This vignette illustrates *AETL* Standard PD-1 C, D, and E; Standard PD-3 A; and Standard PD-7 B. This vignette correlates with *AETL* Standard P-1 A and E; Standard P-2 C; and Standard P-3 F.

Adapted from a vignette written by Michael Daugherty.

Advancing Excellence in Technological Literacy: Student Assessment, Professional Development, and Program Standards

Step 6. Write individual journal entries that explore how the design flaws your team identified in Step 4 coincided with the design flaws the class identified in Step 5. Were they the same? Why or why not? If there were differences, why didn't your team catch them? What is the difference between the consumer's point of view and the corporation's point of view?

Step 7. As a group, solve the design problems.

Step 8. As a group, report back to the class. Record their reactions as notes in your journals.

Step 9. Compare notes with your group. Are the problems solved? Why or why not? If not, work with your group to solve the problems.

Step 10. Individually write a memorandum in your journal to the head of your department detailing the problems with the product and the process your group went through to solve the problems. Make a recommendation about the next step your company should take.

At the conclusion of the activity, the class engaged in discussion to highlight the appropriateness of the learning activity. Topics of discussion included: adaptation of the activity to other content areas or grade levels; coordination with *Standards for Technological Literacy*; opportunities for engagement in cognitive, psychomotor, and affective learning; appropriate student assessment tools and methods; and fashioning activities and lessons into curricula. Teacher candidates were instructed to design a standards-based unit of study that would require elementary students to demonstrate cognitive, psychomotor, and affective knowledge and abilities related to technology. Both formative and summative assessment were to be evident in the content, curricula, and instruction.

Standard PD-4: Professional development will prepare teachers to use instructional strategies that enhance technology teaching, student learning, and student assessment.

Teachers should be prepared to use a variety of instructional strategies in a manner that ensures maximum learning within the laboratory-classroom. Examples include guided discovery, demonstrations, lectures, field trips, simulations, modeling, and others. Professional development should address instructional strategies that are based on learning theory, which focuses on understanding how learning occurs, how it is facilitated, and the content of the curriculum. Teachers should recognize that the goal of instruction is to enhance student learning. Further, teachers must recognize student assessment as another opportunity to enhance and enrich the educational experience for all students. That is, teachers need to learn how assessment is both a learning experience for students and a resource for making instruction more effective.

Correlates with Standard PD-1: To use instructional strategies that enhance technology teaching, student learning, and student assessment, teachers must have knowledge, abilities, and understanding consistent with *STL*.

Correlates with Standard PD-2: To use instructional strategies that enhance technology teaching, student learning, and student assessment, teachers must have educational perspectives on students as learners of technology.

Correlates with Standard P-2: Teachers prepared to use instructional strategies that enhance technology teaching, student learning, and student assessment will be able to implement technology programs that facilitate technological literacy for all students.

Refer to *STL* Standards 1–20: Teachers should present the content identified in *STL* in a manner that allows students to experience technology through design, engineering design, and problem solving (troubleshooting, research and development, invention and innovation, and experimentation).

NOTE: Additional correlations and references at the guideline level can be found in Appendix E.

Guidelines for meeting Standard PD-4 require that professional development providers consistently prepare teachers to

A. Coordinate instructional strategies with curricula. Professional development addresses coordinating instruction with curricula so that technological content is delivered effectively to maximize student learning. Teachers develop strategies for ensuring that instruction is based on a philosophy of teaching rooted in *STL* and develop the knowledge and abilities to deliver instruction that is reflective of *STL* content.

B. Incorporate educational (instructional) technology. Professional development trains teachers in the proper and effective use of educational technology to enhance student learning. Teachers develop abilities to use technological developments, such as computers, audiovisual equipment, and mass media, as tools for enhancing and optimizing the learning environment to assist student development of technological literacy.

C. Utilize student assessment. Professional development addresses assessment as an instructional strategy. Teachers are educated on building student assessment into teaching as a

method for enhancing learning and modifying instruction. Teachers are acquainted with formative (ongoing) assessment to make student thinking and doing visible, enabling teachers, students, and parents to understand student perceptions and thinking. Teachers distinguish between formative and summative (occurring at the end) assessment, recognizing which is appropriate to the learning situation.

Teachers are prepared to develop assessment tools and methods that are student-oriented and learner-friendly. Teachers understand the need for assessment to provide students with opportunities to improve and revise their work and are required to familiarize themselves with "Student Assessment Standards" (chapter 3) of *AETL*. Teachers view assessment as a strategy for helping students monitor their own progress (through self assessment or peer assessment) and attain technological literacy. Teachers learn to utilize student assessment to inform instruction and make positive change to the classroom, to student learning experiences, and to programs.

Description

This workshop is designed to build cross-disciplinary partnerships for planning and creating K–12 curricula that integrate mathematics, science, and technology curricula with *STL*. Curricula development and implementation used long-range goals that included multiple school subjects from kindergarten through the twelfth grade. This vignette illustrates *AETL* Standard PD-3 A, B, C and D and Standard PD-7 B and F. This vignette correlates with *AETL* Standard P-1 A, B, C, and D and Standard P-2 C.

Adapted from a vignette written by James Boe.

K–12 Curriculum Integration Workshop

A professional development four-day workshop was planned for K–12 teachers that focused on integrating mathematics, science, and technology curricula with *STL*. Three national consultants were hired to conduct the workshop, with breakout sessions each day for the K–5, 6–8, and 9–12 grade levels. This workshop was used to develop partnerships among content areas and enhance student learning through integrated hands-on projects, curricular materials, and thematic units. The workshop consisted of 18 teams, and each team consisted of 4 teachers. The first day of the workshop was used to explain the importance of technological literacy and how it can be achieved through interdisciplinary curricula, activities, and partnerships. To stress the importance of collaboration and cooperation, team-building exercises were used with the group to build and enhance skills in communications, work processes, team development, and leadership.

Each day during the remainder of the workshop, the teams participated in breakout sessions led by each of the consultants. The Grades 6–8 and 9–12 teams were introduced to interdisciplinary curricular materials and participated in activities that could be used in the classroom. The teachers discussed how each person on the team could effectively address components of an activity and related materials to create an integrated unit among several disciplines. Once each team had completed the activity and discussion, ideas were shared with the other groups to provide more opportunities for collaboration.

The elementary (Grades K–5) breakout sessions were conducted in a similar manner but focused more on thematic units to help teachers understand how to incorporate the study of technology without adding an additional subject. Consultants explained that thematic units could be used to teach all subjects, using technology activities to link concepts. Teams also prepared classroom materials, project starter kits, and samples that could be used in their classrooms once they returned to their schools.

Throughout each day of the workshop, teams were given opportunities to see demonstrations of different activities and samples of curricular materials from each grade level. These demonstrations helped the teams understand the importance of an articulated curriculum for technology education and the effectiveness of interdisciplinary units. The participants were also given grade level appropriate curricular guides that were developed by the ITEA's Center to Advance the Teaching of Technology and Science (CATTS). The curricular guides were a helpful resource for activities and materials that were presented during the workshop.

The last day of the workshop was dedicated to showing group members how to interpret the standards and benchmarks in *STL* and how to document them in the development of unit plans. Teams also developed implementation plans to use once they returned to their schools. Strategies for implementation were provided during the workshop as suggestions, but each team created a plan that would best fit the strategic plan and curricular policies of their districts.

At the end of the four-day workshop, each participant was given a certificate of completion and awarded two graduate credits from the local university. To continue effective communication between all participants, an attendance list was distributed that included phone numbers, school addresses, and e-mail addresses for each person. This helped build a resource network between teams, participating schools, and the hired consultants for future contacts and questions about curricular development.

Standard PD-5: Professional development will prepare teachers to design and manage learning environments that promote technological literacy.

The learning environment is a major factor in maximizing learning for all students. Teachers must be prepared to design and manage laboratory-classrooms that are learner-centered and adaptable for hands-on experiences. Teachers should be educated to consider the prior knowledge and abilities of learners so they can develop learning environments that are appealing to students and provide a positive space for developing technological literacy. Professional development should prepare teachers to design and manage learning environments that attend to the technological content being taught, the ability levels of the learners, and the reasons for teaching the selected content. Teachers should consider student assessment in the design and management of learning environments. Attention to such details will promote an atmosphere conducive to student learning and teacher instruction.

Correlates with Standard PD-1: To design and manage learning environments that promote technological literacy, teachers must possess knowledge, abilities, and understanding consistent with *STL*.

Correlates with Standard PD-2: To design and manage learning environments that promote technological literacy, teachers must possess educational perspectives on students as learners of technology.

Correlates with Standard P-4: Teachers prepared to design and manage learning environments that promote technological literacy will be able to create and manage learning environments that facilitate technological literacy for all students.

Refer to *STL* Standards 1–20: Teachers should design learning environments that support the development of knowledge and abilities in *STL*.

NOTE: Additional correlations and references at the guideline level can be found in Appendix E.

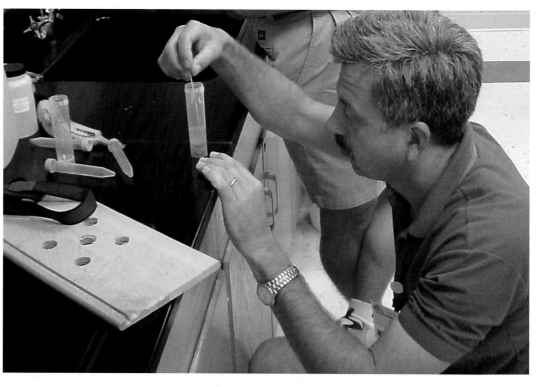

Guidelines for meeting Standard PD-5 require that professional development providers consistently prepare teachers to

A. Design and manage learning environments that operate with sufficient resources. Professional development incorporates the creation of resource-rich learning environments that provide varied educational experiences for students. Teachers learn to draw upon resources in the community, materials within the school, and donations from business and industry. Teachers recognize that recyclable materials may be collected from students and faculty or solicited from local contributors. Teachers understand that activities can be enhanced through technological simulations using tabletop equipment and do not always require large-scale, expensive, industrial equipment.

B. Design and manage learning environments that encourage, motivate, and support student learning of technology. Professional development prepares teachers with strategies to

encourage, motivate, and support students as they learn technology. Teachers are prepared to incorporate hands-on learning that stimulates and reinforces cognition. Teachers are prepared to encourage student innovation and invention as part of developing technological literacy. Design and problem solving are presented as key activities and processes in the study of technology. Teachers learn how to design and manage learning environments that allow students to be creatively engaged in technological activity.

C. Design and manage learning environments that accommodate student commonality and diversity. Professional development prepares teachers to create learning environments that support the needs of all students. Teachers learn to consider student similarities and differences, including interests, cultures, abilities, socio-economic

Advancing Excellence in Technological Literacy: Student Assessment, Professional Development, and Program Standards

backgrounds, and special needs. Teachers are taught to design learning environments that are barrier-free and accommodating to all students.

D. Design and manage learning environments that reinforce student learning and teacher instruction. Through professional development, teachers are prepared to design and manage learning environments that establish high expectations for technological learning and, consequently, establish high expectations for teaching. Teachers learn to devise learning environments that appropriately advance individual student development of technological literacy.

E. Design and manage learning environments that are safe, appropriately designed, and well maintained. Professional development stresses the importance of safe learning environments. Teachers are taught to design and manage barrier-free laboratory-classrooms that enable all students to learn about technology in a safe manner. Teachers learn the importance of regular

equipment maintenance to ensure proper functioning, in accordance with local, district, state/provincial/regional, and national/federal regulations. Teachers recognize the importance of selecting materials and equipment that are appropriate to the developmental abilities of the learners.

F. Design and manage learning environments that are adaptable. As a result of professional development, teachers learn to create learning environments that are flexible and equipped with machines, tools, and materials reflective of the technological content. Teachers recognize that flexible environments facilitate change as demanded by our technological world and enable students to transfer what they have learned from one situation into others. Teachers are educated to be resourceful in making the learning environment adaptable to the content being taught. Teachers know how to implement and use educational (instructional) technology to enhance the learning environment.

Standard PD-6: Professional development will prepare teachers to be responsible for their own continued professional growth.

Pre-service and in-service professional development experiences should prepare teachers to engage in comprehensive and sustained personal professional growth. The most important component affecting the quality of any technology program is the teacher. The faculty in technology programs should be both professionally and technologically prepared to provide students with quality and comprehensive technology learning.

Professional organizations recognize the achievements and contributions of exemplary teachers and programs. In some cases, it may be possible for teachers to initiate political efforts that bring about positive change or influence policy in technology through professional organizations. To remain informed teachers should attend professional conferences at the local, district, state/provincial/regional, national/federal, and international levels, where they network with other teachers to promote the study of technology.

Promoting the study of technology and technology programs is essential, because there is widespread misunderstanding about what the field encompasses. Everyone within the school and the community should be provided with a clear understanding of the importance of technological literacy. This can be accomplished through a planned marketing initiative conducted by teachers and administrators.

> The most important component affecting the quality of any technology program is the teacher.

Correlates with Standard PD-1: Teachers prepared to be responsible for their own professional growth will ensure that they possess knowledge, abilities, and understanding consistent with *STL*.

Correlates with Standard PD-2: Teachers prepared to be responsible for their own professional growth will ensure that they possess educational perspectives on students as learners of technology.

Correlates with Standard PD-3: Teachers prepared to be responsible for their own professional growth will ensure that they possess knowledge and abilities to design and evaluate technology curricula and programs.

Correlates with Standard PD-4: Teachers prepared to be responsible for their own professional growth will ensure that they possess knowledge and abilities to use instructional strategies that enhance technology teaching, student learning, and student assessment.

Correlates with Standard PD-5: Teachers prepared to be responsible for their own professional growth will ensure that they possess knowledge and abilities to design and manage learning environments that promote technological literacy.

NOTE: Additional correlations and references at the guideline level can be found in Appendix E.

Advancing Excellence in Technological Literacy: Student Assessment, Professional Development, and Program Standards

Guidelines for meeting Standard PD-6 require that professional development providers consistently prepare teachers to

A. Assume commitment to self assessment and responsibility for continuous professional growth. Professional development encourages teacher self assessment. Teachers are further encouraged to establish a professional development plan that incorporates maintaining and expanding their professional and technological abilities. Professional development requires teachers to identify goals that guide professionals throughout their careers.

B. Establish a personal commitment to ethical behavior within the educational environment as well as in private life. Professional development

addresses the need for teachers to display ethical behavior. Teachers learn to be role models and are expected to lead students by example, exhibiting ethical behavior at all times. This extends outside the confines of the educational system, as teachers interact with and affect students through their community presence.

C. Facilitate collaboration with others. Professional development emphasizes the significance of collaboration. Teachers develop abilities to effectively collaborate with their peers. Teachers learn that collaboration is an opportunity to share best practices of

what is working and what is not working in the laboratory-classroom. Teachers learn teamwork strategies that enable them to receive ideas from others as well as to share their ideas with others. Professional development offers examples of collaboration to teachers, including observing other teachers in action and participating in discussion forums on technology to receive peer input and advice. Teachers learn that serving as active members of the school instructional staff, sharing in decision-making processes, and participating in technology program advancement are opportunities for collaboration. Teachers are prepared to work with guidance counselors and other personnel, advising them about the importance of technological literacy to students.

D. Participate in professional organizations. Professional development addresses time and resource management issues to prepare teachers for active membership in professional organizations related to technology at the local, district, state/provincial/regional, national/federal, and international levels.

E. Serve as advisors for technology student organizations. Professional development familiarizes teachers with technology student organizations, such as the Technology Student Association (TSA) and the Junior Engineering Technical Society (JETS). Teachers learn how to develop student leadership abilities, encourage and promote student responsibilities, extend student technological abilities, and develop positive social interaction among students through student organizations.

F. Provide leadership in education. Professional development requires that teachers obtain leadership skills to inform others about the study of technology within the school and community. Teachers are prepared to participate in school, community, and political efforts to create positive change in technology programs. Teachers learn strategies for promoting the study of technology as well as for recruiting students to pursue careers in technology teaching.

Advancing Excellence in Technological Literacy: Student Assessment, Professional Development, and Program Standards

Standard PD-7: Professional development providers will plan, implement, and evaluate the pre-service and in-service education of teachers.

Professional growth is essential, as our technological world is ever-changing. Responsibility for the initial stage of pre-service education rests with colleges and universities. This experience must mesh with what is happening in laboratory-classrooms. The interface between college and the classroom is the clinical experience with which many teachers are involved from early in their teacher preparation programs through graduation.

After graduation, responsibility for continuous professional development shifts from the campus to the school district in which the teacher is employed, which may ultimately be a college or university. Every school district, college, and university must be responsible for providing professional development opportunities to technology teachers and other content area teachers to prepare them to deliver content in the study of technology. Such opportunities should include both collaboration with others and formal professional development activities. Professional development for technology teachers and other content area teachers is a continuous, lifelong learning process.

Professional development planning, implementation, and evaluation guides and informs the pre-service and in-service education of teachers. Accordingly, professional development provides opportunities for teachers to build their knowledge and skills, guides teachers in developing instructional strategies, and is continuously evaluated and refined to ensure positive impact on teacher effectiveness, student learning, leadership, and the school community (Loucks-Horsley et al., 1998).

Correlates with Standard PD-1: Professional development is planned, implemented, and evaluated to ensure that teachers are provided with knowledge, abilities, and understanding consistent with *STL*.

Correlates with Standard PD-2: Professional development is planned, implemented, and evaluated to ensure that teachers are provided educational perspectives on students as learners of technology.

Correlates with Standard PD-3: Professional development is planned, implemented, and evaluated to ensure that teachers are prepared to design and evaluate technology curricula and programs.

Correlates with Standard PD-4: Professional development is planned, implemented, and evaluated to ensure that teachers are prepared to use instructional strategies that enhance technology teaching, student learning, and student assessment.

Correlates with Standard PD-5: Professional development is planned, implemented, and evaluated to ensure that teachers are prepared to design and manage learning environments that promote technological literacy.

Correlates with Standard PD-6: Professional development is planned, implemented, and evaluated to ensure that teachers are prepared to be responsible for their own continued professional growth.

Correlates with Standard A-5: Professional development should incorporate student assessment results to guide professional development decisions.

NOTE: Additional correlations and references at the guideline level can be found in Appendix E.

Guidelines for meeting Standard PD-7 require that professional development providers consistently

A. Plan pre-service and in-service education for teachers. Professional development providers coordinate the goals, purposes, content, and context of pre-service and in-service education. Decision making related to professional development is ongoing, and attention is given to the context in which professional development will occur. Effective strategies are considered for implementing the professional development program. A variety of approaches to professional development are planned, including workshops, institutes, curricula development, study groups, case discussions, and immersion in technology. Professional development providers create opportunities for teachers to collaborate with other technology professionals, both within and outside the field of education. College and university programs support teacher candidate involvement in collegiate organizations such as the Technology Education Collegiate Association (TECA). Teachers are involved in the planning of professional development, and the goal of positively influencing student learning is reflected in all activities. Professional development providers coordinate activities to ensure that teacher learning is comprehensive and continuous.

B. Model teaching practices that teachers will be expected to use in their laboratory-classrooms. Professional development providers model teaching practices consistent with the ways teachers will be expected to teach. Professional development is learner-centered, knowledge-centered, assessment-centered, and community-centered. Professional development provides opportunities to learn, practice, and reflect. Professional development providers incorporate opportunities to experience technology through design, problem solving, and invention. Professional development allows for practice in the classroom, with opportunities for teachers to receive feedback and additional practice.

C. Evaluate professional development to assure that the needs of teachers are being met. Professional development providers judge the effectiveness of individual educational opportunities as well as the effectiveness of the overall professional development program. Professional development providers examine the goals and purposes of their instruction to assure that those goals are being met. Program refinement and revision occurs systematically. Input is sought from teachers, other administrators, and policymakers to assure effective professional development. Short- and long-range planning decisions are shared with teachers and other administrators as appropriate. Teachers are held accountable for their learning.

D. Support technology teacher preparation programs that are consistent with state/provincial/ regional and national/federal accrediting guidelines. Professional development providers ensure that technology teacher preparation programs at colleges and universities are accredited using a thorough process that involves state/ provincial/regional and national/federal accrediting guidelines. All technology teacher preparation programs conduct

Advancing Excellence in Technological Literacy: Student Assessment, Professional Development, and Program Standards

self-evaluation processes for national/ federal accreditation. Preparatory programs for elementary teachers and teachers of other content areas require coursework in the study of technology.

E. Provide teacher preparation programs, leading to licensure, that are consistent with *AETL* and *STL*.

Professional development providers in college and university teacher preparation programs base their curricula on *AETL*. The content taught in the teacher preparation program in both the knowledge and ability areas is based on *STL*. Technology teacher preparation programs require methods and strategies for integrating and connecting technology courses of study with pedagogy courses of study and clinical experiences at the baccalaureate degree level. For faculty who plan and conduct professional development at the teacher preparation level, there is continual evaluation of the undergraduate and graduate degree programs to assure quality programs that assist teachers in implementing *STL*.

F. Provide in-service activities to enhance teacher understanding of technological content, instruction, and assessment.

Professional development providers orchestrate and implement a formal program of in-service activities for classroom teachers at school and school district levels. The professional development program informs and educates existing teachers on *STL* and *AETL*. Workshops are conducted on standards-based content, student assessment, and program enhancement. Additionally, class-

room teachers are provided time to attend local, district, state/provincial/ regional, national/federal, and international conferences to further develop their teaching expertise.

G. Obtain regular funding for in-service professional development opportunities.

Professional development providers obtain funding on a regular basis from localities, districts, states/ provinces/regions, universities, and professional organizations. This funding is used to provide in-service on the study of technology to both technology teachers and other content area teachers. Funds are allocated to provide pay for substitute teachers as well as professional leave time for classroom teachers. Alternatives to this may include full department engagement, cross-curricular engagement, rotational engagement, or administrative/faculty teams. Funds are also provided for travel, registration fees, lodging, and meals for teachers attending these activities. Funding is provided to support the alternate licensure of technology teachers by states/provinces/regions. Funds are also available to purchase philosophical, curricular, and instructional materials about technological literacy.

H. Create and implement mentoring activities at both in-service and pre-service levels.

Professional development providers establish and utilize mentoring programs to assist teachers. Mentoring opportunities pair teacher candidates, new teachers, and recertified teachers with experienced teachers, or with teachers in other content areas, to facilitate collaboration. A designated mentor provides assistance to new teachers and recertified teachers during the first three years following certification or recertification.

Advancing Excellence in Technological Literacy: Student Assessment, Professional Development, and Program Standards

Facilitating Collaboration

School administrators interested in enhancing their cross-curricular technology program (see glossary for further elaboration on *cross-curricular technology program*) invited teachers to attend a case discussion to investigate collaboration as a possible technique for increasing awareness of the technology program and promoting it to the community. The purpose of the case discussion was made clear to participants. Their goal was to develop an action plan to facilitate collaboration among elementary, middle, and high school teachers and local technology professionals. Participants were provided the following example, detailing an online collaboration project completed by three geographically distant schools to design and construct 3-D plastic puzzles:

> This online collaboration was successfully completed between schools in New York, Nevada, and California. The student participants were technology students in Grades 7–12. Students from the three states combined their efforts and resources to design and manufacture 3-D puzzles using computer aided design (CAD) (Nevada), computer numerical control (CNC) (California), and computer graphics (New York).
>
> Through participation in this multi-school project, students developed skills in mathematics, science, technology, and language arts. In the beginning, students introduced themselves by sending letters and photos. Then a student-developed website was established, complete with message board and chat room, where students from the three schools could post their efforts on the shared project.
>
> In the course of this project, students developed abilities to communicate electronically, share resources, and develop skills in problem solving and critical analysis, in accord with *STL*. Students documented project progress on the website. This project engaged students in a practical experience while encouraging the integration of multiple subjects and application of integrated knowledge and processes. The project promoted integrated learning and fostered equal participation. The electronic environment was inviting to all participants, inclusive of diversity among students. This was a learner-focused project with clear connectivity between expectations, standards, processes, and assessment. This project provided experience in planning, research, development, testing, critiquing, presentation, and reflection. The experiences were enhanced with the application of technology and electronic documentation.
>
> Students faced and overcame many practical challenges during the course of the project. For example, during the development of the first student-designed 3-D puzzle, the Nevada school was told by the California school that they purchased 1/8″ Plexiglas™ for the puzzles. With that information, the puzzles were designed with 1/8″ slots. The CAD data were then sent to California, and the pieces were cut out using a laser CNC. The puzzles arrived in New York with slots that were so large the puzzle would not stay together when assembled. When New York used a digital caliper on the plastic, it measured 0.100″ (not 0.125″) in thickness. This information was communicated to Nevada, and the students began problem solving. They decided to

Description

This case discussion was organized by administrators interested in promoting programs for the study of technology. Teachers were involved in planning a collaborative effort among elementary, middle, and high school teachers and local technology professionals. An example of a multi-school collaboration project was provided. This vignette illustrates *AETL* Standard PD-6 A and C and Standard PD-7 A and F. This vignette correlates with *AETL* Standard P-1 C, D, J, and K and Standard P-5 A, C, D, and F.

Adapted from a vignette written by Donna Matteson.

Advancing Excellence in Technological Literacy: Student Assessment, Professional Development, and Program Standards

scale the entire puzzle from 1" to 0.8", which solved the problem of having to resize all of the slots on each of the 25 puzzle parts. Communication was the key to the success of this project. E-mail capability overcame the time difference between the East and West Coasts.

The outcome of this project was that the educational experience was enhanced through the collaborative effort and the application of current technology to a practical project. At the conclusion of the project, all students participated in a live videoconference, where they discussed the experience. They discussed the skills in communication, problem solving, and critical analysis they had developed through the project. Educational outcomes included, but were not limited to, the following: students gained experience in geometry, mathematical coordinates, physics, research, writing, design, graphics, communications, and manufacturing.

This was an educationally sound and rewarding experience for both teachers and students. We hope it will serve as a model to inspire others. Any school could model this effort. The first step would be to identify teachers interested in participating in a shared project. The NY/NV/CA network was established at an ITEA conference. However, contacts could be made through teacher centers as well as local, state, or national organizations. This project is not limited to subject area or grade level. This project received recognition as a runner up in the 2001 National Semi-Conductor Innovators Award for programs utilizing the Internet to pursue creative endeavours. The website address is available for review at *http://www.bnet.org/hvsd/manufacturing*.

Participants were given ten minutes to read and reflect on the example. They were instructed to brainstorm a list of steps to foster the collaboration. Following the ten-minute time period, the action plan development process was initiated. Administrators used a list of guidelines to engage teachers in discussion and incorporate the ideas that were generated during the brainstorming session. The discussion was conducted in an organized manner so that all teachers were provided ample time to ask questions and voice opinions and concerns. To create an action plan, administrators sought teacher input regarding the following:

- **Define the vision for the collaborative effort.** Administrators felt that the collaborative effort would enhance teacher knowledge and abilities by providing opportunities for teachers to interact with technology professionals from local businesses and industries. It was also viewed as an opportunity for teachers to work together in and out of their respective disciplines and grade levels. Student learning could be enhanced if partnerships were developed and opportunities were provided to students within and outside their respective classrooms. Administrators were interested in learning teacher perspectives on the significance of such collaboration.
- **Outline the collaborative effort.** Clear identification of what the collaborative effort would be within the school district was detailed with input from the teachers and administrators.
- **Build support for the collaborative effort.** Administrators sought teacher expertise in determining most effective strategies for receiving "buy in" from school faculty and the community.

- ■ **Identify a "champion" for the collaborative effort.**
  Administrators felt it was important to identify a "champion" or "cheerleader" for the effort to increase faculty and community interest. Advice from teachers was sought to determine appropriate person(s) or group(s).
- ■ **Create a collaborative team.** Advice regarding appropriate individuals to serve on a collaborative team was gathered from teachers. Consideration was given to teacher expertise, including content area and grade level to ensure diverse representation.
- ■ **Acquire administrative support.** Methods for ensuring support from administration at all levels (school, district, community) were discussed, including channels of communication.
- ■ **Allocate resources.** Necessary resources and appropriate sources of funding were identified.
- ■ **Publicize and promote.** A procedure was discussed to market the study of technology.

Program
Standards

The standards in this chapter describe effective and appropriate practices to be used by teachers and administrators (including supervisors) as well as by local, district, state/provincial/regional, and national/federal entities to provide the continuous study of technology throughout student academic careers. These program standards are aligned with *Standards for Technological Literacy: Content for the Study of Technology* (*STL*) (ITEA, 2000a). They are developed to be implemented in conjunction with *STL* as well as with the student assessment and professional development standards included in *Advancing Excellence in Technological Literacy: Student Assessment, Professional Development, and Program Standards* (*AETL*). Therefore, program standards are of optimal use when curricula and instruction have incorporated the concepts and principles identified in *STL*. **These standards apply to the study of technology in technology programs and other content area programs**. The ultimate goal is for all students to achieve technological literacy.

Note: The standards in this chapter are not intended to address programs for computer literacy or programs for educational (instructional) technology.

Administrators are those professionals who manage any aspect of the educational system, including supervisors or teachers as appropriate.

This chapter has separate guidelines aimed at teachers and administrators. As a result, there is some redundancy between the guidelines for teachers and those for administrators.

The cross-curricular technology program refers to everything that affects student attainment of technological literacy implemented across grade levels and disciplines.

Definition of Program

For the purposes of this document, program refers to everything that affects student learning, including content, professional development, curricula, instruction, student assessment, and the learning environment, implemented across grade levels. *Programs for the study of technology* support student attainment of technological literacy through technology programs as well as other content area programs. In other words, programs for the study of technology are cross-curricular in nature. The *technology program* incorporates the study of technology across grade levels as a core subject of inherent value. The *cross-curricular technology program* manages the study of technology across grade levels and disciplines.

Scope of Programs for the Study of Technology

The program standards address the system that supports the comprehensive study of technology across grade levels and disciplines within a school or school district. In preparing the program guidelines, the TfAAP staff noted that some guidelines were directed especially to teachers while others were directed toward administrators. With this in mind, this chapter has guidelines aimed at each of these groups. As a result, there is some redundancy between the guidelines for teachers and those for administrators.

Guidelines directed at teachers provide guidance to technology teachers and other content area teachers responsible for facilitating instruction in the study of technology. While many of the guidelines apply to dedicated technology laboratory-classrooms, all teachers should be aware of the requirements for creating learning environments that support the development of technological literacy.

Guidelines directed at administrators provide guidance for establishing a cross-curricular technology program that incorporates the study of technology in all classrooms of all grade levels, including but not exclusive to the technology laboratory-classroom. The cross-curricular technology program should be managed by administrators. It should support the study of technology through the technology program as well as other content area programs. Documented curricula based on *STL* should be established and in use by teachers. Licensed teachers, who plan and facilitate learning, should be employed to deliver the most comprehensive content for the study of technology. While student attainment of technological literacy is primarily the responsibility of the elementary teacher in Grades K–5 and the technology teacher in Grades 6–12, technological literacy for all students is a goal that transcends the technology laboratory-classroom. Correspondingly, a cross-curricular technology program must be in place to support technological literacy development in technology programs as well as in other content area programs, across Grades K–12.

In keeping with current research on how students learn (NRC, 2000), these standards integrate the total educational experience from Grades K–12 so that students are provided with continuous technology learning throughout their educational experience. The management of programs for the study of technology must ensure a well-managed and effective system for developing student technological literacy. Administrative support is necessary to ensure that technology learning opportunities are available to students in technology laboratory-classrooms as well as other content area classrooms.

Programs for the study of technology must be continually evaluated for quality. Evaluation instruments should be aligned with the program standards in this chapter and provide accountability to all constituents involved with and interested in the quality study of technology.

Program Permeability

The vision behind the program standards calls on teachers, administrators, and policymakers to perpetuate interchange between elements of the program, including content, professional development, curricula, instruction, student assessment, and the learning environment, in all areas of learning. The standards and guidelines of chapters 3, 4, and 5 of *AETL* are overlapping in nature to facilitate such interchange.

Audiences for "Program Standards"

Primary audiences:

- Teachers
- Administrators (including Supervisors)

Other targeted audiences:

- Policymakers
- State/Provincial/Regional Accreditation Boards
- National/Federal Accreditation Boards
- Business and Industry
- General Public

These program standards apply to the study of technology in technology programs and other content area programs.

The management of programs for the study of technology must ensure a well-managed and effective system for developing student technological literacy.

Advancing Excellence in Technological Literacy: Student Assessment, Professional Development, and Program Standards

Standard P-1: Technology program development will be consistent with *Standards for Technological Literacy: Content for the Study of Technology (STL)*.

Technology program development should be based on the nationally developed *STL*, which provides the content ingredients for the study of technology. *STL* defines what the study of technology in Grades K–12 will be, but it does not dictate curricula or how the content of programs should be structured, evaluated, or organized across grade levels. This task is left—as it should be—to the schools, school districts, and states/provinces/regions.

An increasing number of voices are calling for the inclusion of technology as a core discipline in elementary, middle, and high schools. In other words, technology programs should support the development of technology as a subject of inherent value, a core subject that develops technological literacy, not only as a subject that facilitates the understanding of other content areas. Curricula are major components of the program, as they specify how the content identified in *STL* is structured across grade levels. Curricula should be in the form of written documents, and every effort should be made to keep them current. This is extremely important in the study of technology, where the dynamic nature of the field results in constant change.

The development and implementation of the cross-curricular technology program should support the study of technology in various content areas across Grades K–12. In other words, dedicated technology laboratory-classrooms as well as science, mathematics, social studies, language arts, and other content area classrooms should be part of the cross-curricular technology program. Technology teachers and other content area teachers should work with administration to ensure that the study of technology occurs in a comprehensive, articulated fashion across grade levels and disciplines.

> **An increasing number of voices are calling for the inclusion of technology as a core discipline in elementary, middle, and high schools.**

Correlates with Standard P-2: Technology program development consistent with *STL* should be implemented in a manner that facilitates technological literacy for all students.

Correlates with Standard P-3: Technology program development consistent with *STL* should be evaluated in a manner that ensures and facilitates technological literacy for all students.

Correlates with Standard P-4: Technology program development consistent with *STL* should include learning environments that facilitate technological literacy for all students.

Correlates with Standard A-1: Technology programs developed to be consistent with *STL* will utilize student assessment that is consistent with *STL*.

Correlates with Standard A-4: Technology programs developed to be consistent with *STL* will utilize student assessment that reflects practical contexts consistent with the nature of technology.

Correlates with Standard PD-1: For technology program development to be consistent with *STL*, teachers must be prepared with knowledge, abilities, and understanding that is consistent with *STL*.

Correlates with Standard PD-3: For technology program development to be consistent with *STL*, teachers must be prepared to design and evaluate technology curricula and programs.

Refer to *STL* Standards 1–20: *STL* identifies the knowledge and abilities students must develop in their progression toward technological literacy in Grades K–12.

NOTE: Additional correlations and references at the guideline level can be found in Appendix E.

Guidelines for teachers appear below. Guidelines for administrators begin on page 74.

Guidelines for meeting Standard P-1 require that the teacher(s) responsible for the technology program(s) consistently

A. Align program content with *STL*.
Teachers ensure program content is aligned with the standards and benchmarks of the five main categories identified in *STL*: The Nature of Technology, Technology and Society, Design, Abilities for a Technological World, and The Designed World. Programs also comply with other school district, state/provincial/regional, and national/federal standards.

B. Align program content with school district, state/provincial/ regional, and national/federal standards in other academic areas.
Teachers incorporate *STL*, as well as other content area standards, into technology programs. Nationally developed standards include (but are not limited to):

- *National Science Education Standards* (NRC, 1996)
- *Benchmarks for Science Literacy* (AAAS, 1993)
- *Principles and Standards for School Mathematics* (NCTM, 2000)
- *Geography for Life: National Geography Standards* (GESP, 1994)
- *National Standards for History* (NCHS, 1996)
- *Standards for the English Language Arts* (NCTE, 1996)
- *National Educational Technology Standards for Students* (ISTE, 2000)

C. Plan and develop the program across disciplines. Teachers infuse technology programs with interdisciplinary linkages between technology and all school subjects, including science, mathematics, social studies, language arts, and other content areas. Accordingly, nationally developed standards in other content areas are considered in developing technology programs (see bulleted list in the previous guideline narrative).

D. Plan and develop the program across grade levels. Teachers consider student developmental levels and design technology programs that are continuous and seamless from elementary schools through middle and high schools. Thus, students experience a holistic, integrated, practical approach to technology and technological literacy. Technology programs are documented, not just discussed. Further, technology programs

Advancing Excellence in Technological Literacy: Student Assessment, Professional Development, and Program Standards

detail the ways in which post high school experiences can provide opportunities for graduates to delve more extensively into technological studies. Such linkages are made to both formal and informal education and include workplaces, professional careers, the military, mass media and entertainment outlets, book and periodical publishers, and museums, among others.

E. Assure that the program incorporates suitable cognitive, psychomotor, and affective learning elements. Teachers empower all students to attain technological literacy. Opportunities for students to gain and demonstrate knowledge and abilities related to technology are integrated to facilitate student understanding (i.e., knowing + doing = understanding). Teachers encourage students to become independent learners by integrating perspective, empathy, student self assess-

ment, and student peer assessment with technological activities. Simulations or real applications require students to demonstrate their knowledge and understanding of the positive and negative impacts and consequences in the development and use of technology. Technological activities are varied and representative of practical experiences, requiring students to think critically and make decisions.

F. Promote adaptability for program enhancement. Teachers keep technology programs up-to-date with state/provincial/regional and national perspectives based on the adoption of continuous-improvement models. Short- and long-range strategic planning is detailed, continuously reviewed, current, and oriented toward the future. Technology programs are dynamic, reflective of the evolving nature of technology.

Guidelines for meeting Standard P-1 require that administrators responsible for establishing the cross-curricular technology program consistently

G. Stipulate that content be aligned with *STL*. Administrators require teachers to align the study of technology with the standards and benchmarks of the five main categories identified in *STL*: The Nature of Technology, Technology and Society, Design, Abilities for a Technological World, and The Designed World. Programs for the study of technology also address other school district, state/provincial/regional, and national/federal standards.

H. Mandate instruction in the study of technology as part of the core educational experience for all students. Administrators require teachers to incorporate the study of technology into daily instruction of all students. Advancement and graduation requirements incorporate technological literacy. Scheduling formats are adjusted to allow time for all students to study technology, both in technology laboratory-classrooms as well as in other content area classrooms.

I. Advocate content that complements school district, state/provincial/regional, and national/federal standards in other academic areas. Administrators require teachers to incorporate *STL*, as well as other content area standards, into their programs. Nationally developed standards include (but are not limited to):

■ *National Science Education Standards* (NRC, 1996)
■ *Benchmarks for Science Literacy* (AAAS, 1993)
■ *Principles and Standards for School Mathematics* (NCTM, 2000)
■ *Geography for Life: National Geography Standards* (GESP, 1994)
■ *National Standards for History* (NCHS, 1996)
■ *Standards for the English Language Arts* (NCTE, 1996)
■ *National Educational Technology Standards for Students* (ISTE, 2000)

J. Assure that the study of technology occurs across disciplines. Administrators expect technology teachers and other content area teachers to work together to promote the study of technology in all school subjects. Programs acknowledge the interdisciplinary linkages that technology provides between all school subjects, including science, mathematics, social studies, language arts, and other content areas. Accordingly, nationally developed standards in other content areas are considered in the development of the cross-curricular technology program (see bulleted list in the previous guideline).

K. Assure that the study of technology occurs across grade levels. Administrators consider student developmental levels and ensure that the study of technology is continuous and seamless from elementary schools through middle and high schools. Programs provide students with holistic, integrated, practical approaches to technology and technological literacy.

L. Promote adaptability to enhance the study of technology. Administrators insist that the study of technology occurs in a manner that is up-to-date and consistent with state/provincial/regional and national perspectives. Short- and long-range strategic planning is detailed, continuously reviewed, current, and oriented toward the future. Programs in the cross-curricular technology program are dynamic, reflective of the evolving nature of technology. They also reflect the practical nature of technology, providing opportunities for students to know and do technology.

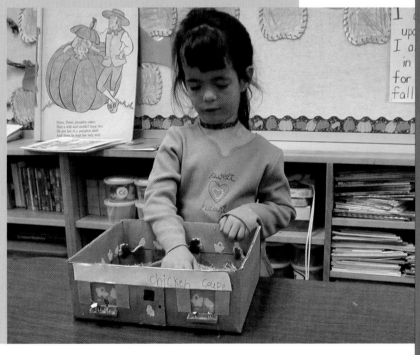

Advancing Excellence in Technological Literacy: Student Assessment, Professional Development, and Program Standards

Description

This transformation from Industrial Arts to Technology Education was successfully made due to administrator and stakeholder support. This vignette illustrates *AETL* Standard P-1 G, K, and L and Standard P-5 D, F, G, I, and K. This vignette correlates with *AETL* Standard A-5 A and C; Standard PD-3 A and D; and Standard PD-7 F.

Adapted from a vignette written by W. David Greer, DTE.

A Transformation, Not A Reformation:

The Need for District-Wide Vision and Stakeholder Buy In

The Fort Worth Independent School District successfully made the transformation from Industrial Arts to Technology Education in 17 middle schools and 12 high schools from 1989 to 1994. These programs and additional programs were transformed once again in 2000 to reflect the latest changes in the study of technology. It is anticipated that another transformation will be on the horizon in 2005 or 2006.

First, the vision for the program was shared by district administrators, supervisors, the school board, teachers, and community leaders (especially those businesses and industries in the area that hired the students). This vision specifically delineated the need for transformation, not simple reformation of the old program. Simply adding updated technology equipment, for example, would not accomplish the vision. It is important to note that there was not total buy in by all stakeholders; the decision makers, both administratively and financially, were the primary forces behind successful transformation.

Next, a plan was developed that included the mission statement, short- and long-range goals, evaluation standards, program selection, curricula, retrofitting of facilities and, perhaps most importantly, all aspects of teacher training. To help teachers attain the vision, local administrators and supervisors shared their ideas. Then, teachers were exposed to existing programs, sent to state and national conferences and workshops, and finally provided with intensive training for every step of the implementation process. Teacher in-service began a year prior to implementation of the program.

Once the program was implemented, follow-up was conducted. Follow-up included continual in-service of teachers; updating curricula, instructional materials, and software; evaluation, feedback, and modifications to the program; and public relations to illustrate program success to stakeholders. Providing students with opportunities to share their experiences with family and friends was an effective strategy for promoting the technology program to the community. Support from the community was also solicited through educator participation in district-wide activities that promoted other programs in the school and showed how the technology program supported such programs as science, mathematics, social studies, language arts, and other content areas.

Standard P-2: Technology program implementation will facilitate technological literacy for all students.

Implementation of programs for the study of technology should be accomplished by licensed technology teachers in dedicated technology laboratory-classrooms and by other content area teachers in regular classroom settings. Support from management is crucial. All teachers must be well prepared in pedagogy. Technology teachers and other content area teachers must possess technological knowledge and abilities. The licensure requirements for all teachers should be based on state/provincial/regional and national/federal accreditation guidelines. Instruction of technology should be based on *STL* and school district, state/provincial/regional, and national/federal standards in other academic areas.

Teachers of all school subjects, including technology, must be provided with sustained professional development to keep them abreast of the dynamic, technology-related subject matter. Instruction should comply with current research on how students learn technology. Instruction should also advance curricular goals and student needs.

Correlates with Standard P-1: Technology program implementation that facilitates technological literacy for all students requires development that is consistent with *STL*.

Correlates with Standard P-4: Technology program implementation that facilitates technological literacy for all students requires learning environments that facilitate technological literacy.

Correlates with Standard PD-2: For teachers to implement technology programs that facilitate technological literacy for all students, they must be provided with educational perspectives on students as learners of technology.

Correlates with Standard PD-3: For teachers to implement technology programs that facilitate technological literacy for all students, they must be prepared to design and evaluate technology curricula and programs.

Correlates with Standard PD-4: For teachers to implement technology programs that facilitate technological literacy for all students, they must be prepared to use instructional strategies that enhance technology teaching, student learning, and student assessment.

Refer to *STL* Standards 1–20: Implementation of technology programs should be consistent with *STL* and provide students opportunities to experience technology through design, engineering design, and problem solving (troubleshooting, research and development, invention and innovation, and experimentation).

NOTE: Additional correlations and references at the guideline level can be found in Appendix E.

Advancing Excellence in Technological Literacy: Student Assessment, Professional Development, and Program Standards

Guidelines for teachers appear below. Guidelines for administrators begin on page 79.

Guidelines for meeting Standard P-2 require that the teacher(s) responsible for the technology program(s) consistently

A. Provide instruction that is consistent with research on how students learn technology. Teachers incorporate the effects of student commonality and diversity, assist students in becoming effective learners, and use informative student assessment in the classroom, consistent with "Student Assessment Standards" (chapter 3) of *AETL*. Teachers use the tools and materials of educational (instructional) technology properly and effectively to enhance student learning.

B. Provide instruction that is designed to meet curricular goals and student needs. Teachers develop curricular guides and materials using multiple sources of information, including research, student assessment data, state and national professional association resources, and input from stakeholders. Curricular guides are used to direct the selection and delivery of courses of study that support the development of technological literacy for all students. Teachers design and use instructional strategies based on curricular guides that incorporate prior learning and experiences of students yet avoid unnecessary repetition.

C. Design and implement curricula that enable all students to attain technological literacy. Teachers implement programs using curricula that enable students to learn from multiple (knowing and doing) perspectives. Teachers use the latest standards-based curriculum development methods. Implementation of curricula is consistent with *STL*, providing students with opportunities to apply design abilities in solving practical problems. Curricula and instructional strategies are evaluated on a systematic basis.

D. Develop student leadership opportunities. Teachers provide co- and extra-curricular opportunities to develop student leadership through student organizations, enhancing what students learn in technology programs. For example, teachers support the Technology Student Association (TSA), which provides co-curricular educational experiences that enhance leadership skills and enrich student learning about technology, and the Junior Engineering Technical Society (JETS), which offers students a number of services and activities to enhance technological literacy.

Guidelines for meeting Standard P-2 require that administrators responsible for establishing the cross-curricular technology program consistently

E. Employ licensed teachers to deliver technology content.

Administrators employ specialized technology teachers to serve as the key people to facilitate student technological literacy in the school. All teachers complete accreditation procedures that incorporate state/provincial/regional and national/federal accreditation guidelines for their specialty areas. Licensure may be obtained through an undergraduate teacher preparation program or through alternative licensure methods. Technology teachers and other content area teachers possess knowledge and abilities consistent with *STL* and "Professional Development Standards" (chapter 4) of *AETL*. Professional development is provided to existing teachers, enabling them to comply with updated licensure requirements.

F. Support sustained professional growth and development of all educators.

Administrators establish annual funding to support the study of technology by providing professional development activities, enabling existing teachers and other educators to remain current with technology content. Administrators organize mentoring activities for new teachers and student teachers. Administrators provide teachers with opportunities to collaborate with other educators about technological literacy. Adequate time is provided within school schedules for teachers to pursue professional development. Administrators expect teachers to adhere to a high standard of ethical behavior both inside and outside the classroom. Incentives are offered to teachers to encourage their involvement in and advisement of student technology organizations. Administrators expect teachers to provide leadership for their students, incorporating positive views toward teaching and learning into daily instruction.

G. Encourage instruction that is consistent with research on how students learn technology.

Administrators expect all teachers to accommodate for student commonality and diversity, assist students in becoming effective learners, and use informative student assessment in the classroom, consistent with "Student Assessment Standards" (chapter 3) of *AETL*. Administrators encourage teachers to use the tools and materials of educational (instructional) technology properly and effectively to enhance student learning.

H. Advocate instruction that is designed to meet curricular goals and student needs.

Administrators require classroom teaching practices to be consistent with curricular goals and student needs. Resources are made available to support the development of curricular guides and documents using multiple sources of information, including research, student assessment data, state and national professional association resources, and input from stakeholders. Administrators require teachers to design instructional strategies based on curricular guides that incorporate prior learning

> Educators are professionals involved in the teaching and learning process, such as teachers or administrators.

Advancing Excellence in Technological Literacy: Student Assessment, Professional Development, and Program Standards

and experiences of students yet avoid unnecessary repetition. Administrators provide resources to accomplish this task.

I. Commit to the recruitment of technologically competent teachers.
Administrators support active, continuous recruitment of technology teachers at the local, district, and state/provincial/regional levels. Resources are made available to support teacher recruitment efforts. Recruitment begins as early as middle or high school. Administrators encourage teachers to observe students in class to identify and recruit candidates for undergraduate technology teacher preparation programs. Administrators encourage students to pursue careers as technology teachers. Administrators also encourage the community and local business and industry to establish scholarships for students who plan to return to their school districts as technology teachers.

J. Encourage all teachers to develop student leadership opportunities.
Administrators encourage all teachers to provide co- and extra-curricular opportunities to develop student leadership through student organizations. For example, the Technology Student Association (TSA) provides co-curricular educational experiences that enhance leadership skills and enrich student learning about technology, and the Junior Engineering Technical Society (JETS) offers students a number of services and activities to enhance technological literacy.

Standard P-3: Technology program evaluation will ensure and facilitate technological literacy for all students.

Each school, school district, and state/province/region should evaluate its programs to verify that the study of technology is occurring in technology laboratory-classrooms as well as in other content area classrooms in a manner consistent with the program standards. Student achievement can be interpreted only in light of the quality of the program that students experience. The variety and quality of student assessment tools and methods based on *STL* is of critical importance in the validity of decisions made in program evaluation. Essentially, the study of technology must be evaluated to ensure that all students achieve technological literacy.

Those responsible for the study of technology should report its successes as well as its failures to all stakeholders. Most localities, districts, and states/provinces/regions require some type of accountability for the overall school program, including establishing the study of technology. Accreditation agencies at the state/provincial/regional and national/federal levels provide an excellent formal review process. Advisory committees are an excellent way to receive input on the quality of programs. The results of these evaluations should be shared with stakeholders through formal reports, internal and external reviews, articles in local newspapers, spots on local television shows, parent-teacher open houses, student organizations, and by other means. Revisions based on program evaluations should occur, as the nature of technology is continuously changing.

Effective technological study inspires all students to become keenly interested in technology as an inherent human ability and trait. Educational experiences in technology should challenge students to pursue careers in technology as, for example, engineers, architects, technicians, and technology teachers, among many other professions.

Correlates with Standard P-1: Technology program evaluation that ensures and facilitates technological literacy for all students must be developed consistent with *STL*.

Correlates with Standard P-5: Technology program evaluation that ensures and facilitates technological literacy for all students requires development that is consistent with *STL*.

Correlates with Standard A-1: Technology program evaluation requires student assessment that is consistent with *STL*.

Correlates with Standard A-2: Technology program evaluation requires student assessment that is explicitly matched to its intended purpose.

Correlates with Standard A-3: Technology program evaluation requires student assessment that is systematic and derived from research-based principles.

Correlates with Standard A-4: Technology program evaluation requires student assessment that reflects practical contexts consistent with the nature of technology.

Correlates with Standard A-5: Technology program evaluation requires student assessment that incorporates data collection for accountability, professional development, and program enhancement.

Correlates with Standard PD-3: For teachers to be able to evaluate technology programs, they must be prepared to design and evaluate technology curricula and programs.

Refer to *STL* Standards 1–20: Evaluation of technology programs should ensure and facilitate technological literacy for all students in accordance with the standards in *STL*.

NOTE: Additional correlations and references at the guideline level can be found in Appendix E.

Guidelines for teachers appear below. Guidelines for administrators begin on page 84.

Guidelines for meeting Standard P-3 require that the teacher(s) responsible for the technology program(s) consistently

A. Develop and utilize evaluation that is consistent with standards and guidelines in "Program Standards." Teachers work with administrators to assure that external reviews of programs for the study of technology are performed in effective and efficient manners. Evaluations consider, among other things, whether students are provided with relevant, rigorous, and contextual connections to the technological world. Input is sought from parents, other caregivers, and the community at large to facilitate well-rounded technological studies. Advisory committees are formed, comprised of informed and qualified persons. Community input from parents, business and industry leaders, local engineers, and interested citizens also serves as a valuable resource to strengthen programs.

B. Implement and use systematic, continuous evaluation. Teachers collect and use data for program evaluations to plan and refine content. For example, evaluation data are used to prepare activities that are incorporated into curricular courses of study, modules, units, or lessons. Teachers collect evaluation data in a systematic and continuous manner.

C. Evaluate instruction on a regular basis. Teachers evaluate, reflect upon, and learn from their own practice. Teachers openly seek to understand which plans, decisions, and actions are effective in helping students learn, and which are not. The process of continued refinement of teaching is based on ongo-

Advancing Excellence in Technological Literacy: Student Assessment, Professional Development, and Program Standards

ing evaluation of instructional strategies. Teachers collect data in their classrooms to assist them in making these decisions.

D. Plan for program revision.

Teachers use program evaluation criteria to guide them in self assessment. Short- and long-range planning are documented and used to make programs comply with the needs revealed by evaluation. Strategic plans assist teachers with long-range program revisions.

E. Accommodate for student commonality and diversity.

Teachers design program evaluation criteria that accommodate student similarities and differences, including interests, cultures, abilities, socio-economic backgrounds, and special needs. Teachers provide access to students who, traditionally, have not been served by technology programs. Technology programs accommodate the needs of all students.

F. Utilize effective student assessment.

Teachers evaluate programs using multiple methods to gather data about student progress, including portfolios, project assessments, peer evaluations, rubrics, participation in class, reports, and group work, among others. Both formative and summative student assessment are aligned with curricular goals, and the resulting data from student assessment tools and methods are used to plan and revise programs. Technology teachers and other content area teachers are familiar with "Student Assessment Standards" (chapter 3) of *AETL*. Student assessment measures both knowledge and abilities. Teachers are concerned about preventing isolated assessment results from becoming representations of the larger educational system. Accordingly, when using student assessment results to impact program decisions, teachers pay particular attention to the original purpose(s) and intended audience(s) of the assessment tool or method to ensure that results are not interpreted out of context.

Advancing Excellence in Technological Literacy: Student Assessment, Professional Development, and Program Standards

Guidelines for meeting Standard P-3 require that administrators responsible for establishing the cross-curricular technology program consistently

G. Assure that evaluation is consistent with standards and guidelines in "Program Standards."
Administrators evaluate the programs. In addition, external reviews are conducted by groups charged with performing such evaluations. Administrators assure that external reviews are performed in effective and efficient manners. Evaluations consider, among other things, whether students are provided with relevant, rigorous, and contextual connections to the technological world in technology laboratory-classrooms as well as in other content area classrooms. Administrators seek input from parents, other caregivers, and the community at large to facilitate a comprehensive evaluation. Administrators form advisory committees, comprised of informed and qualified persons. Administrators seek community input from parents, business and industry leaders, local engineers, and interested citizens.

H. Employ systematic, continuous evaluation. Administrators use evaluation data to plan and refine the study of technology in technology laboratory-classrooms and in other content area classrooms. Administrators ensure that evaluation data are collected in a systematic and continuous manner by teachers, other administrators, and external sources. Administrators require teachers to conduct systematic, continuous evaluation to assure that activities, lessons,

units, modules, and courses of study provide students opportunities to attain technological literacy.

I. Encourage evaluation of instruction on a regular basis.
Administrators encourage teachers to evaluate, reflect upon, and learn from their own practice. Administrators routinely observe classroom instruction and offer teachers feedback and guidance to ensure the utilization of instructional strategies that promote student attainment of technological literacy. Administrators support teachers as they seek to understand which plans, decisions, and actions are effective in helping students learn, and which are not. The process of continued refinement of teaching is based on ongoing evaluation of instructional strategies. Administrators expect teachers to collect data in their classrooms to assist them in making decisions and refine their teaching.

J. Plan for program revision.
Administrators prepare evaluation criteria to guide teachers in self assessment. Short- and long-range planning are documented and used to assure that programs comply with the needs revealed by evaluation. Strategic plans are developed to assist with long-range revisions. Administrators seek input from teachers regarding short- and long-range planning decisions and discuss strategic plans with the faculty as appropriate.

Data-Based Decision Making

Ms. Smith taught technology for six years at the high school level. After reviewing her curriculum guide, Ms. Smith noticed that the content of her course related to energy and power was outdated and needed to be revised. A fellow teacher mentioned workshops provided by the Technology for All Americans Project Standards Specialists to inform educators about *Standards for Technological Literacy* (*STL*) and provide them with strategies for implementing the standards in the laboratory-classroom.

Ms. Smith attended a workshop, where she learned about *STL* and strategies for implementing *STL* into her curriculum. Upon returning from the workshop, Ms. Smith decided to design an end-of-the-course examination aimed at assessing student attainment of the *STL* standards and benchmarks related to energy and power. She tested her students to determine a baseline for student learning prior to her planned curriculum revision.

Ms. Smith used the student assessment data, *STL*, and the program standards in *AETL* to begin revising her curriculum. As she worked on this task, she realized that other teachers in her region might also want to revise their curricula. With this thought in mind, she contacted the local university to ask her former professor if any systematic reform was taking place to update energy and power curricula. Because he indicated there was not, Ms. Smith collaborated with the professor to involve other teachers in the curriculum revision.

Several teachers in the region expressed an interest in joining Ms. Smith's efforts to revise the technology program curricula. Recognizing that curricula demands constant revision when content is based on a field as dynamic as technology, the teachers sought funding for a three-year period to allow multiple revisions. With the support of administration, they ultimately obtained funding through the State Department of Education to use student assessment data on technological literacy as the basis for making curricular revisions to all content area programs.

The first re-design occurred during the summer. A student assessment instrument was developed to guide future revisions. After the first re-design, curricula were taught for a year, and students were assessed at the conclusion of the year. The results of the testing, along with data gathered prior to curricular revision, guided the second revision of the curricular materials. Ms. Smith and her colleagues met periodically to collaborate on curricular revisions.

During the second summer, revisions were made based on data gathered during the previous year and in accordance with standards in *STL* and *AETL*. Student test results guided the curricular refinement efforts and allowed curricula to be designed to satisfy student-learning needs. The curricula were used to instruct students for a second year, and during the third summer, revisions were made again. While Ms. Smith's original intent was to develop a standards-based curriculum for a single course, she stimulated development of a framework that allowed teachers to collect and use data related to student learning of technology to improve instruction, curricula, and student assessment.

VIGNETTE

Description

This technology program revision effort began with one teacher and became a systematic, continuous evaluation method that allowed teachers to revise curricula, instruction, and student assessment tools to support program revisions and ensure accountability. While the case presented is specific to the technology laboratory-classroom, teachers of other school subjects can apply the concepts detailed in the passage to the revision of their curricula, instruction, and student assessment tools, promoting effective delivery of technology content. This vignette illustrates *AETL* Standard P-3 A, B, C, D, and F. This vignette correlates with *AETL* Standard A-1 A; Standard A-3 C; Standard A-5 C; and Standard PD-6 C.

Adapted from a vignette written by John M. Ritz, DTE.

Advancing Excellence in Technological Literacy: Student Assessment, Professional Development, and Program Standards

Standard P-4: Technology program learning environments will facilitate technological literacy for all students.

In the 35th American Council on Industrial Arts Teacher Education (ACIATE) Yearbook entitled, *Implementing Technology Education Yearbook* (1986), Richard Henak and Richard Barella assert that the environment where technology is taught should include both "physical" and "social" elements. The physical environment used for the study of technology consists of the laboratory-classroom, equipment, materials and supplies, and services that support teacher instruction and student learning. The social environment is the atmosphere for learning, and it should be supportive, friendly, and energizing for all learners. Learning is influenced in fundamental ways by the environment in which it takes place.

Many laboratory-classrooms are ill-equipped to accommodate the standards-based study of technology. Administrators should support technology teachers and other content area teachers by providing learning environments conducive to the study of technology. Such environments include dedicated technology laboratory-classrooms as well as other content area classrooms that enhance student understanding of the technological world.

As our technological society advances, learning environments, resources, and support mechanisms will be in constant change. Current, well-maintained, up-to-date equipment and tools are mandatory for the study of technology. At the elementary grade levels (K–5) and in content areas other than technology education, schools do not need separate rooms for student activities; in many respects, it is advantageous to study technology in an integrated classroom environment, as it facilitates long-range studies and connections between school subjects. In middle and high schools, dedicated technology laboratory-classrooms should be provided to satisfy the requirements of the cross-curricular technology program, which supports the study of technology in technology laboratory-classrooms as well as in other content area classrooms.

Correlates with Standard P-1: Technology program learning environments that facilitate technological literacy for all students must incorporate development that is consistent with *STL*.

Correlates with Standard P-2: Technology program learning environments that facilitate technological literacy for all students are required for the implementation of technology programs.

Correlates with Standard PD-2: For teachers to develop learning environments that facilitate technological literacy, they must be provided with educational perspectives on students as learners of technology.

Correlates with Standard PD-5: For teachers to develop learning environments that facilitate technological literacy, they must be prepared to design and manage learning environments that promote technological literacy.

Refer to *STL* Standards 1–20: Learning environments should facilitate technological literacy for all students in accordance with the standards in *STL*.

NOTE: Additional correlations and references at the guideline level can be found in Appendix E.

Guidelines for teachers appear below. Guidelines for administrators begin on page 88.

Guidelines for meeting Standard P-4 require that the teacher(s) responsible for the technology program(s) consistently

A. Create and manage learning environments that are supportive of student interactions and student abilities to question, inquire, design, invent, and innovate. Teachers design attractive, motivating, stimulating, and nurturing learning environments, where academic risk taking is encouraged and rewarded and students are not afraid to make mistakes and learn from them. Teachers design activities with an understanding spirit and in ways to promote excitement. The environment is learner-centered, and attention is given to what is taught, why it is taught, and what level of technological literacy is being pursued. The learning environment encourages student innovation, problem solving, and design, and it establishes expectations for student learning and teacher instruction. Teachers also use other environments in the community and at business and industry locations to enhance student learning.

B. Create and manage learning environments that are up-to-date and adaptable. Teachers efficiently manage a capital equipment budget line in the school budget for technology programs. Teachers obtain consumable materials and supplies in sufficient quantity and quality to achieve program goals. Teachers design or modify the learning environment to accommodate equipment, tools, materials, and unique instructional strategies that represent current and future technologies using a continuously updated long-range plan.

Teachers take advantage of new developments and make the best use of current resources and systems. Teachers work with various constituents to help create the optimal learning environment, including administrators, advisory committees, parents, policymakers, business and industry leaders, legislators, and others.

C. Implement a written, comprehensive safety program. Technology teachers assist in preparing a written and comprehensive safety program for the study of technology. This safety program is implemented to ensure safe conditions and practices. Teachers design and maintain the learning environment to comply with local, district, state/provincial/regional, and national/federal specifications, codes, and regulations. Teachers upgrade the learning environment based on the results of external safety inspections. Teachers provide students with safe equipment and tools, adapting them as necessary to accommodate the needs of all students.

Advancing Excellence in Technological Literacy: Student Assessment, Professional Development, and Program Standards

D. Promote student development of knowledge and abilities that provides for the safe application of appropriate technological tools, machines, materials, and processes.
Teachers expect students to demonstrate acceptable knowledge, abilities, and attitudes of safe practices and rules through written and performance-based tests as well as in-class behavior. Consequently, by the time students graduate from high school, they are able to work with an assortment of tools, materials, sophisticated equipment, and other resources. Teachers develop student abilities to synthesize knowledge and processes and apply them to new and different situations.

E. Verify that the number of students in the technology laboratory-classroom does not exceed its capacity. Teachers verify that the workstations or resource capacities in laboratory-classrooms are appropriate for the number of students in technology programs. Teachers ensure that the number of students on any given day does not compromise the safety of the learning environment. Teachers acknowledge that in some cases, a workstation will accommodate a single student, while in others, like modular environments, typical workstations may serve two or more students. Teachers notify administrators of unsafe learning environments so necessary improvements can be made.

Guidelines for meeting Standard P-4 require that administrators responsible for establishing the cross-curricular technology program consistently

F. Provide learning environments that are designed to facilitate delivery of *STL* and satisfy "Program Standards." Administrators provide technologically-appropriate learning environments to teachers. Administrators ensure that learning environments are created and managed based on the content in *STL*. They also ensure that the learning environment is in compliance with the standards and guidelines in *AETL*. The learning environment is resource-rich and incorporates a variety of technologies. The learning environment is equipped for the use of educational (instructional) technology. It accommodates both student commonality and diversity in a positive manner, providing specially designed or modified equipment and tools as appropriate to the needs of students. Administrators provide dedicated technology laboratory-classrooms at the middle and high school levels that are managed by technology teachers. Administrators provide learning environments supportive of the study of technology to elementary teachers and to teachers of other content areas.

G. Provide learning environments that are safe, up-to-date, and adaptable. Administrators allocate funds to provide consumable materials and supplies in sufficient quantity and quality to teachers to ensure program goals are achieved. Administrators create a capital equipment budget line in the budget for programs for the study of technology.

Administrators provide resources to ensure that the learning environment is designed to accommodate equipment, tools, materials, and unique instructional strategies. Funding allows teachers to take advantage of new developments and make the best use of current resources and systems. Administrators ensure the laboratory-classroom is a safe learning environment. Administrators require teachers to evaluate the safety of the learning environment in compliance with local, district, state/provincial/ regional, and national/federal specifications, codes, and regulations and report their findings.

H. Ensure that the number of students in a dedicated technology laboratory-classroom does not exceed its capacity. Administrators ensure that the workstations or resource capacities in dedicated technology laboratory-classrooms are appropriate for the number of students in the program. Administrators ensure that the number of students on any given day does not compromise the safety of the environment.

I. Provide elementary school classrooms with adequate physical space for teaching technology. Administrators support the study of technology in a regular classroom at the elementary school level. Administrators provide ample space for students to do activities in a safe manner. Additionally, adequate physical space is provided in or near the classroom for the safe storage of equipment, tools, individual/group projects, materials, and supplies.

J. Provide dedicated technology laboratory-classrooms in middle and high schools with a minimum allotment of 100 square feet per pupil, inclusive of safe ancillary space. Administrators provide dedicated space at the middle and high school levels for technology laboratory-classrooms. Administrators provide adequate space for students to work individually as well as collectively in the study of technology and to display both work in progress and finished work. Ancillary space exists for the safe and convenient storage of projects, group products, and materials needed to study technology.

Advancing Excellence in Technological Literacy: Student Assessment, Professional Development, and Program Standards

Advancing Excellence in Technological Literacy: Student Assessment, Professional Development, and Program Standards

Description

These educators describe how the study of technology looks in their classrooms and what classroom learning environment is most effective to help students achieve technological literacy. As these educators describe classrooms at various grade levels and from varied content area perspectives, their responses reflect implementation of a cross-curricular technology program. This vignette illustrates *AETL* Standard P-1 C, D, E, G, J, and K and Standard P-4 A, B, D, F, I, and J.

Contributions by:
Bonnie B. Berry,
Janis Detamore, Thomas Kaiser,
and Melvin Robinson.

The Study of Technology:

A Cross-Curricular Perspective

Question: What does the study of technology look like in your classroom?

Response: As a kindergarten teacher, I am given content knowledge that I am responsible to teach to my students. Children's Engineering or Design Technology is not something extra added onto that teaching task, it is a teaching strategy that integrates the core curriculum areas. When handed a design brief, my students become actively involved and embrace their learning. They learn to become divergent and critical thinkers as they creatively solve real-world problems. The end product instills pride and confidence, and their learning is relevant—ensuring longer retention. Design Technology puts the FUN into teaching and learning.—*Bonnie B. Berry, Kindergarten Teacher*

Response: Technology education in the 2nd grade classroom looks inviting to all ages. In any given lesson, students are planning, designing, measuring, building and creating, observing, sharing, changing, sometimes failing, and possibly starting all over again. Students use tools such as saws, drills, and hammers to accomplish the challenges presented to them. The building starts after the planning part of the portfolio is completed. Reflection and sharing are the final aspects of this learning loop. The students take ownership and assume responsibility for their learning. By becoming designers, their discoveries are more meaningful and relevant to real-life situations.—*Janis Detamore, 2nd Grade Teacher*

Response: I prefer to use long-term projects that incorporate all of the aspects of what we are learning. That way students are able to see and do all of the steps that go into a project. I also feel it is important to stress process over product. Not all projects will work or look perfect, but if the student has learned all of the processes, steps, and skills related to the area of study, they will have a better chance at being successful in projects and challenges to come.—*Thomas Kaiser, 11th and 12th Grade Technology Education Teacher*

Response: In the state of Utah, we are using the ITEA's *Standards for Technological Literacy: Content for the Study of Technology* as the backbone for our Technology and Engineering programs. Technological literacy is the main focus in all of our middle school/junior high school programs. At the high school level, we are also focusing on introducing students to the world of engineering.—*Melvin Robinson, Technology and Engineering Specialist, Utah State Office of Education*

Question: What classroom learning environment would be most effective in facilitating technological learning?

Response: My classroom contains many resources such as Lasy®, Legos®, and Gears® for the children to design, build, test, and evaluate their own creations. Design briefs generate innovative ideas, which the very young student sometimes lacks the ability to carry out if not given support. Support can be an adult having the strength to punch holes in a plastic container. During one activity, the students designed and built a monkey cage and wanted an alarm on the door. Support was necessary to secure the correct switch and wire it. Students use computers and digital cameras when creating technology log reports.—*Bonnie B. Berry, Kindergarten Teacher*

Response: The classroom learning environment has to first and foremost be a safe place where students have learned how to correctly use the tools. It is a place where listening and observing your peers helps you in your own planning and implementation. It is a place where everyone is excited about his or her own ideas and stays on task in order to accomplish his or her goals. For example, when creating their "perfect chair," students worked through many of the content areas and didn't even realize it, because they were having too much fun. We talked about and experienced firsthand how to make the chairs unique. We also learned and implemented geometry, scale, measuring, spatial relationships, writing persuasive paragraphs, and oral expression. My job is to state the challenge, set the limitations, and then fade into the background to help and encourage while the students take control of their own learning.—*Janis Detamore, 2nd Grade Teacher*

Response: The best learning environment for project-based learning is a laboratory setting. Here instructional strategies such as demonstration and practice can be used. Often, drawings on a white board or short discussions can lead to a detailed demonstration. Hopefully, a good demonstration will help the students ask good questions and prepare them to do the task them-selves. Once they have acquired the knowledge and abilities necessary to perform the assigned task, they will be able to transfer their understanding to other activities and projects.—*Thomas Kaiser, 11th and 12th Grade Technology Education Teacher*

Response: The best facility would have three parts. First, a classroom with desks, where discussions, lectures, and knowledge processing can take place; second, a clean area with 5 to 10 computer learning stations, equipped with current computers and software that can be used to help teach technological literacy; and third, a well-equipped general production laboratory where students can get their hands dirty building models, proto-types, and other applied activities that promote learning. Our motto here in Utah is "Hands On, Minds On Education."—*Melvin Robinson, Technology and Engineering Specialist, Utah State Office of Education*

Standard P-5: Technology program management will be provided by designated personnel at the school, school district, and state/provincial/regional levels.

The quality of management in the study of technology is a key factor in the success or failure of the system. Management personnel must understand the differences between technology, technology education, technological literacy, and educational technology as well as their interrelationships. *Technology* is the innovation, change, or modification of the natural environment (world) to satisfy perceived human wants and needs. *Technology education* is the study of technology; it provides an opportunity for students to learn about processes and knowledge that are needed to solve problems and extend human capabilities. The standards-based study of technology leads to *technological literacy. Educational technology* uses technologies as tools to enhance the teaching and learning process (ITEA, 2002a).

All management personnel, including teachers and administrators, must support the contribution of technological study in advancing technological literacy for all students in Grades K–12. All management personnel should ensure that the study of technology, under their leadership, complies with *STL* and utilizes the standards and guidelines in *AETL* for student assessment, professional development, and program enhancement in the schools. Those who establish programs for the study of technology must provide curricular, instructional, philosophical, and fiscal support for technological studies to teachers.

Correlates with Standard P-1: Technology program management must be provided to confirm that technology program development is consistent with *STL*.

Correlates with Standard P-2: Technology program management must be provided to confirm that technology program implementation facilitates technological literacy for all students.

Correlates with Standard P-3: Technology program management must be provided to confirm that technology program evaluation ensures and facilitates technological literacy for all students.

Correlates with Standard P-4: Technology program management must be provided to confirm that technology program learning environments facilitate technological literacy for all students.

Correlates with Standard A-5: Technology management personnel will utilize student assessment data to guide program enhancement decisions.

Correlates with Standard PD-3: To manage technology programs, teachers must be prepared to design and evaluate such programs.

Refer to *STL* Standards 1-20: Technology program management must be provided to ensure that technology program content is consistent with *STL*.

NOTE: Additional correlations and references at the guideline level can be found in Appendix E.

Advancing Excellence in Technological Literacy: *Student Assessment, Professional Development, and Program Standards*

Guidelines for teachers follow. Guidelines for administrators begin below.

Guidelines for meeting Standard P-5 require that the teacher(s) responsible for the management of the technology program(s) consistently

A. Develop and use action plans based on *STL*. Teachers develop and use action plans based on *STL* that incorporate program mission statements, goals, short- and long-range strategic planning, organization, evaluation, and responsibilities. Teachers incorporate mission statements and goals into long-range technology program action plans.

B. Maintain data collection for accountability. Teachers are accountable to the stakeholders. Teachers make external evaluation results public to the constituents in the community. Accountability systems are sensitive to the needs of the community.

C. Market and promote the study of technology. Teachers market technology programs to the community, helping to increase public understanding about technology. Advisory committees are very helpful in this process. Student involvement in organizations such as the Technology Student Association (TSA) and Junior Engineering Technical Society (JETS) are available to assist. Teachers develop relationships with local businesses and industries to solicit understanding and support. Teachers promote technology programs and technological literacy as essential components of education to parents, the local school board, and civic and economic development groups.

Note: While each of the following guidelines suggests general means of meeting the standard, users should refer to Table 6 (p. 96) for suggested responsibilities of schools, school districts, and states/provinces/regions.

Guidelines for meeting Standard P-5 require that administrators responsible for the management of the cross-curricular technology program consistently

D. Develop and use action plans based on *STL*. Administrators develop and use action plans based on *STL* that incorporate program mission statements, goals, short- and long-range strategic planning, organization, evaluation, and responsibilities. Programs for the study of technology are in place, with mission statements and goals as part of the long-range plan.

E. Maintain data collection for accountability. Administrators are accountable to the stakeholders. The results of external evaluation are made public and are shared with all of the constituents in the school and the community. Accountability systems are sensitive to the needs of the community.

F. Market and promote the study of technology. Administrators market the study of technology to the community, helping to increase public understanding about technology. Administrators may use advisory committees to help in this process. Student involvement in organizations such as the Technology Student Association (TSA) and Junior Engineering Technical Society (JETS) are available to assist. Administrators develop relationships with local businesses and industries to solicit understanding and support. Administrators promote technological literacy as an essential component of education to parents, the local school board, and civic and economic development groups.

G. Provide funding, support, and resources to accomplish missions, goals, and curricular objectives. Administrators identify funding sources, and multi-year budget proposals are prepared based upon improvements targeted by programs for the study of technology. Administrators advocate for and allocate funds for professional development,

maintenance, resources, and planning. Legislative budget requests support strategies for technological literacy. Policies and procedures that support equipment, supplies, and professional development are developed and utilized. Standard accounting and inventory practices are shared no less than quarterly with instructional staff.

H. Align technology programs with state/provincial/regional accreditation systems. Administrators employ accountability systems that evaluate and measure how the study of technology aligns with state/provincial/regional standards for technological literacy and satisfies program standards identified in this chapter. These results indicate program compliance with *STL* and *AETL*. Administrators use *STL* and *AETL* to judge the quality and effectiveness of technology programs.

I. Establish articulated and integrated technology programs district wide. Administrators articulate and

integrate the study of technology district wide. Articulation ensures that students develop the knowledge and abilities identified by *STL* in a consistent, progressive manner from kindergarten through Grade 12. Administrators encourage technology teachers to actively promote the study of technology in a manner that encourages students to acknowledge the interdisciplinary linkages that technology provides among all school subjects.

J. Establish and utilize a management system. Administrators use data and observations to monitor, evaluate, and manage the study of technology. These data are collected, analyzed, transmitted, stored, maintained, and reported to stakeholders. The mandates of state/provincial/regional policy are observed by administrators in the management of the study of technology.

K. Support professional technology organization engagement by teachers and management personnel. Administrators participate—and encourage teachers to participate—in committees and professional organizations related to technology for the purposes of technological literacy improvement and continuity. Management personnel provide leadership in professional organizations, collaborating with technology teacher preparation programs. All management personnel keep abreast of the

latest thinking in the study of technology and encourage teachers to do the same.

L. Provide resources and opportunities to support technology teachers and other content area teachers in the teaching and learning process. Administrators maintain manageable teacher schedules and class sizes. Necessary resources are provided by administrators for the successful operation of programs for the study of technology. Resources and opportunities for all teachers to engage in program implementation are also provided. Administrators establish and enforce policies and practices to encourage support for teachers and the teaching and learning process. Resources are also provided by administrators for the continued professional development of all educators concerned with advancing student technological literacy.

Advancing Excellence in Technological Literacy: Student Assessment, Professional Development, and Program Standards

Table 6. Guidelines for Standard P-5: School, School District, and State/Provincial/Regional Realms of Responsibility

Standard P-5: Technology program management will be provided by designated personnel at the school, school district, and state/provincial/regional levels.

Guidelines for meeting Standard P-5 require that administrators responsible for the management of the cross-curricular technology program consistently	School	School District	State/Provincial/Regional
D. Develop and use action plans based on *STL*.	Write a school improvement plan.	Write a locally defined plan with mission statement and goals.	Write a statewide/province-wide/region-wide framework with vision/mission statements.
E. Maintain data collection for accountability.	Conduct evaluation on a regular schedule.	Use data and/or observations to improve programs.	Observe the mandates of state/provincial/regional policy in the evaluation of technological studies.
F. Market and promote the study of technology.	Promote the study of technology to parents and the local school board. Establish an advisory committee to promote the study of technology within the community.	Promote program to community and civic and economic development groups. Promote the study of technology via local media. Establish liaison to local advisory committee.	Develop and employ marketing techniques to promote the study of technology at the state/provincial/regional levels.
G. Provide funding, support, and resources to accomplish missions, goals, and curricular objectives.	Identify funding resources and plan multi-year budget based on program improvements.	Allocate funds for professional development resources and planning.	Request state/provincial/regional and national/federal legislative budget allocations to support strategies for technological literacy. Adopt policies and procedures that support equipment, supplies, and professional development.
H. Align the technology program with state/provincial/regional accreditation systems.	Observe the mandates of school policy in the evaluation of the program.	Observe the mandates of district policy in the evaluation of the program.	Observe the mandates of state/provincial/regional policy in the evaluation of the program.
I. Establish articulated and integrated technology programs district wide.	Schedule and assign staff. Provide resources.	Advocate professional development and program development.	Provide statewide/province-wide/region-wide leadership through effective communication, professional development, and program development.
J. Establish and utilize a management system.	Develop and use a management system for the school program.	Establish and utilize district-wide management to provide direction and administration to the program.	Establish and utilize a state/provincial/regional management system to guide and direct the program.
K. Support professional technology organization engagement by teachers and management personnel.	Participate in committees and professional organizations within and beyond the school.	Provide leadership in professional organizations at the district, state/provincial/regional, and national/federal levels.	Provide leadership in professional organizations at state/provincial/regional and national/federal levels. Collaborate with technology teacher preparation programs in states/provinces/regions.
L. Provide resources and opportunities to support technology teachers and other content area teachers in the teaching and learning process.	Maintain manageable schedules and class sizes. Provide necessary resources for the operation of the program.	Provide resources and opportunities for curriculum development and program implementation.	Establish and enforce policies and practices to encourage local and district administrators to support teachers and the teaching and learning process.

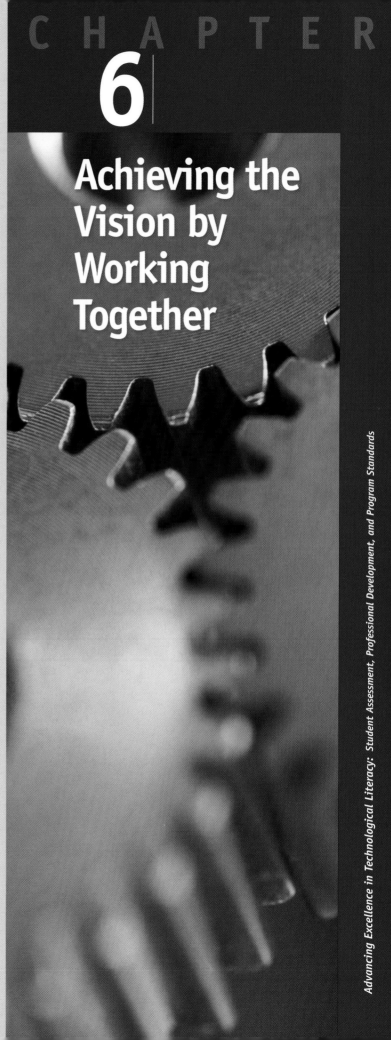

Achieving the Vision by Working Together

Visualize a laboratory-classroom where students are engaged in the study of technology. The standards described in *Standards for Technological Literacy: Content for the Study of Technology* (*STL*) (ITEA, 2000a) are reflected in the learning activities. Imagine all of the students with varied prior experiences and abilities working collectively, in pairs, and individually to learn about the technological world in which they live. Students are actively engaged, trying out solutions to technological problems. They revisit prior solutions and retest ideas using new information. They are curious, ask questions, and accept the responsibility for developing technological literacy. Student assessment is varied, providing information for students to adjust their learning and for teachers to adjust their instruction. It is an active environment full of enthusiasm for learning.

Picture teachers seeking professional development opportunities to remain current in the study of technology and confident about utilizing *Advancing Excellence in Technological Literacy: Student Assessment, Professional Development, and Program Standards* (*AETL*) and *STL* in the laboratory-classroom. Schools support the study of technology and have faculties that work together to empower students. Elementary teachers, technology teachers, and other content area teachers work together to integrate content and educational activities to make learning more interesting and meaningful.

Imagine administrators, policymakers, parents, business and industry leaders, and the community at large working together to create environments that promote the study of technology and support teacher and student growth. Time and resources are provided, enabling teachers to educate and students to learn. Institutions of higher education support teacher preparation and professional development in compliance with professional development standards. Professional and student organizations, such as the International Technology Education Association (ITEA), the Technology Education Collegiate Association (TECA), the Council for Technology Teacher Education (CTTE), the ITEA Council of Supervisors (ITEA-CS), the Technology Education Children's Council (TECC), the Technology Student Association (TSA), and the Junior Engineering Technical Society (JETS) provide leadership, resources, professional development, and opportunities for teachers and students that improve the study of technology and the development of technological literacy for all.

Making technological literacy a reality for all students requires a strong system of support for content (*STL*), student assessment, professional development, and programs (*AETL*).

Recognizing the Challenge

The study of technology is offered in most schools in a variety of formats. Some states/provinces/regions offer the study of technology as an elective, while others provide it as part of core requirements. If the study of technology is to undergo the acceptance and implementation necessary to bring about technological literacy for all students, policies must support the vision inherent in *STL* and *AETL,* consistently requiring all students to study technology from kindergarten through Grade 12.

Local, district, and state/provincial/regional entities are generally more influential in promoting the study of technology in a school system than any other group. It is important that local policymakers, state and local school boards, and state/provincial/ regional and federal legislators become familiar with the goals of *STL* and *AETL*. Implementing the standards and developing technology programs for Grades K–12 will require content, professional development, curricula, instruction, student assessment, and learning environments that enable all students to develop technological literacy.

Support from professionals teaching technology is vital to the realization of the vision. Using *STL* and *AETL* as a basis for modifying instruction, teachers can highlight the importance of the study of technology and the value of technological literacy.

AETL identifies standards necessary to support the study of technology. Many systems influence the study of technology, including government, the public sector, and professional organizations and societies. These systems must work together to deliver quality education related to the study of technology. Day-to-day activities in the laboratory-classroom are directly and indirectly affected by the decisions that are made by the individuals that comprise these systems. Therefore, it is imperative that all those involved in the study of technology are aware of the recommendations being made and the need for technologically literate students. Systems must support the vision contained in *STL* and *AETL*.

If the study of technology is to undergo the acceptance and implementation necessary to bring about technological literacy for all students, policies must support the vision inherent in STL and AETL, consistently requiring all students to study technology from kindergarten through Grade 12.

Roles and Responsibilities

In conjunction with *STL* and *AETL*, the following need to be involved in the development, implementation, and evaluation of technology programs:

- Teachers
- Teacher Educators/Higher Education
- Resource Developers
- School Administrators and Policymakers
- Technology Students and Student Organizations
- Parents, Other Caregivers, and Communities
- Business and Industry
- Museums
- Professional Organizations
- Researchers

Teachers

Technology teachers and other content area teachers must develop and maintain the technological and pedagogical knowledge necessary to teach students. *STL* and *AETL* provide the necessary roadmap to help them move forward. Collaborating with colleagues, taking advantage of professional development opportunities that fit their learning needs, and consulting with professionals on how to enhance their programs are some of the methods that teachers may use to help create learning opportunities where few exist. Technology teachers and other content area teachers are responsible for what happens in the laboratory-classroom and can directly influence how students perceive and accept learning. Technology teachers and other content area teachers must help their students feel confident and engaged in developing technological literacy. They must use all resources available to meet this goal. At the elementary level, technology should be taught in the regular classroom. Although elementary teachers may initially feel unqualified to teach technology, with quality in-service they can integrate technological concepts across the curriculum. At middle and high school levels, technology teachers have a major responsibility to advance technological literacy. Other content area teachers can also confirm and support the necessity for technological literacy. Utilizing *STL* and *AETL*, these teachers will enable students to learn about the rich interdisciplinary relationships between technology and other school subjects, such as science, mathematics, social studies, language arts, and other content areas.

Teacher Educators/Higher Education

Higher education faculties have significant influence on the teaching of technology, primarily through their work with teacher candidates but also through effective in-service of existing teachers. Teacher preparation and higher education programs must teach educators how to implement the standards in *STL* and *AETL*. The first few years of a teacher's career are critical to his or her persistence in teaching and to his or her disposition toward continued professional development. In-service programs must address *AETL* and help teachers implement *STL*. College and university administrators are

Advancing Excellence in Technological Literacy: Student Assessment, Professional Development, and Program Standards

encouraged to provide support and philosophical leadership for reform and to work closely with K–12 education to provide effective in-service. Those who educate technology teachers should review and revise undergraduate and graduate degree programs using *AETL* as the basis for teaching technology. Furthermore, strategies should be designed and implemented for incorporating state/provincial/regional and national/federal accrediting guidelines to help implement and accredit teacher preparation programs, including innovative methods to recruit and retain teachers. Teacher preparation faculty should assist in developing and reforming the study of technology in elementary, middle, and high schools. Collaboration with other professional development providers, veteran teachers, engineers, and other technologists will help demonstrate to new teachers the value of continued professional growth.

Resource Developers

If the study of technology is to be effective, the time in the school day devoted to technology, as well as the instructional materials, facilities, equipment, and other parts of technology programs, must be appropriate and current. In particular, instructional materials and support documents produced by resource developers should be reflective of *STL* and *AETL*. If policies are enacted without regard for the resources needed to implement *AETL*, schools, teachers, and students are placed in impossible positions. The design and structure of curricular materials and learning systems for the study of technology produced by resource developers must reflect the vision that all students can develop technological literacy. For schools to meet the standards in *STL* and *AETL*, technological literacy by all students must be viewed as a primary purpose and a worthy goal, and policies must support the vision.

School Administrators and Policymakers

Beyond the laboratory-classroom, school administrators—principals, supervisors, directors of instruction, superintendents, and others—must recognize the importance of technological literacy for all students and support the study of technology. School administrators must actively pursue support from business and industry. To that end, school administrators and policymakers can provide support and work to develop policies that are congruent with *AETL* while allowing for local adaptation. These policies need to have specific characteristics including, but not limited to:

- Coordination within and across the school community.
- Sufficient time to provide continuity to bring about change.
- Resources necessary to promote program reform.
- Review and evaluation to meet the changing needs of teachers and students.
- Equitable opportunities for all students to truly overcome challenges and have the opportunity to achieve technological literacy.

Technology Students and Student Organizations

Students who study technology (technology students) often work on technological problems, innovations, and inventions. When curricula are stimulating, challenging, and rewarding, students are encouraged to become actively involved in the development of technological literacy. If students are committed to developing technological literacy, they will do their part by engaging seriously with the material and striving to make connections between technology and content in other school subjects that will enhance their learning. Technology students need to communicate their ideas and understandings to their teachers, better enabling teachers to design instruction to address student misconceptions or difficulties. Technology students need to take advantage of the resources available to them to help answer their questions, enhance their learning, and improve their technological literacy. As students look to potential careers in technology, they can begin to discover the requirements for those careers and investigate what technology courses of study they should pursue to help them prepare for their futures.

The Technology Student Association (TSA) provides co-curricular educational experiences that enrich student development of technological literacy. To further that goal, TSA chapters are encouraged to use *AETL* in developing teacher preparation materials, new activities, and competitive events.

Preparing teachers and advisors with the standards put forth in *AETL* could enhance other student groups offering services and activities to students, including Student Council and FFA. At the collegiate level, the Technology Education Collegiate Association (TECA), a university-based organization for teacher candidates, can incorporate *AETL* into its teacher preparation activities.

Parents, Other Caregivers, and Communities

Parents, other caregivers, and communities should be invited to participate in examining and improving programs for the study of technology. Everyone needs to be aware of the goals and reformations proposed in *AETL*. When parents and their communities understand the value of the study of technology and developing technological literacy, they can be invaluable in convincing children, friends, and others of the need to learn more about technology and to take the study of technology seriously. If parents and others are not aware of the value of the study of technology, they can halt carefully planned revision and reform. *AETL* is written to encourage dialogue and commitment to improving the study of technology for all students. It is the responsibility of the educational system to inform parents, other caregivers, and communities about the goals and objectives of the technology program. This empowers everyone to participate knowledgeably.

Business and Industry

It is vital that business and industry leaders and professionals at the local, district, state/provincial/regional, and national/federal levels become more involved in preparing students for future endeavors, especially in developing technological literacy. Business and industry leaders and professionals have the resources and expertise to help implement *STL* and *AETL*. They should be encouraged to work closely with school, school district, and state/provincial/regional educators to improve the study of technology. Providing their expertise to teachers, students, and technology programs, business and industry leaders can aid in developing high quality, relevant, hands-on experiences that will empower students and augment their learning.

Museums

Museums and science/technology centers can play an important role in the implementation of technological literacy. Citizens of all ages are afforded informal education through exhibits, interactive displays, and other programs at museums and science/technology centers. Museums and science/technology centers should work closely with the technology profession in the future to further these opportunities.

Professional Organizations

Engineers, designers, architects, technologists, scientists, and other professionals and their organizations, as well as the International Technology Education Association (ITEA) and teacher associations, such as the National Council of Teachers of Mathematics (NCTM), the National Science Teachers Association (NSTA), and the American Association for the Advancement of Science (AAAS), can provide national and regional leadership and expertise in supporting the reform efforts and the implementation of *STL* and *AETL*. Professional organizations that serve as champions of technological literacy for all, such as the National Academy of Engineering (NAE), the National Academy of Sciences (NAS), the Institute of Electrical and Electronic Engineers (IEEE), the American Society of Mechanical Engineers (ASME), and the Industrial Designers Society of America (IDSA), will not only benefit society in general but also the professions they represent. Programs that lead to careers in these professions include the K–12 educational community. Technological literacy will benefit these professions in a number of ways. For example, as more students receive high-quality instruction in technology more will be likely to select one of the many technological professions available and pursue future studies in a technological field.

Researchers

Quality programs are vital to the health of technology as a discipline, and the profession of technology teachers has a clear stake in this enterprise. Because few studies have examined K–12 technology programs, there is an acute need for additional research about technology. In particular, research is needed that explores the specific ways in which students learn technology and how the study of technology enhances the student educational experience. This research will be important in providing information to policymakers that will reinforce the value of including technology in today's schools. Furthermore, research is needed to move *AETL* forward and to provide support and direction for future revisions. Active research by teachers and administrators is necessary. They may study the current assessment tools or consider how the development of new

Research is needed that explores the specific ways in which students learn technology and how the study of technology enhances the student educational experience.

curricula based on *STL* and the incorporation of up-to-date assessment methods affect how well students meet the standards. Research in this area will help to improve "Student Assessment Standards" (chapter 3) of *AETL*. Likewise, research in professional development and program enhancement is necessary to prevent disjointed or haphazard efforts. A research agenda that addresses "Professional Development Standards" (chapter 4) and "Program Standards" (chapter 5) of *AETL* will be invaluable in developing opportunities to advance the teaching and learning of technology.

School, school district, state/provincial/regional, and national/federal curricular frameworks and standards need ongoing examination and revision. An accepted and refined research agenda is necessary to help reform efforts be timely and effective.

Putting *Advancing Excellence in Technological Literacy* into Action

The standards in chapters 3, 4, and 5 offer perspectives to guide policymakers. If the study of technology or the ideas conveyed in *STL* are not student accessible, student development of technological literacy will be haphazard and happenstance. Technology teachers and other content area teachers need to have learning environments that enable students to learn and teachers to know what students learn. The following highlights each of the chapters, showing how the standards can help shape answers to important questions about the study of technology.

Is assessment aligned with instructional goals and reflective of "Student Assessment Standards?" Assessment is a fact of life in education. Large-scale assessment tools and methods have become a major concern to many educators. Technology teachers and other content area teachers are understandably concerned when large-scale tests concentrate on cognitive learning and leave out the psychomotor and affective domains.

Assessment tools and methods must be in alignment with *STL* and incorporate "Student Assessment Standards" (chapter 3) of *AETL*. If they are not aligned, and if they do not reflect the school and community goals for the study of technology, teachers and students are left in a risky position. If teachers have adopted *STL* and *AETL*, then satisfying the sometimes opposing roles of school, school district, state/provincial/regional, and national/federal assessment policies and procedures can be challenging. "Teaching to the test" becomes a reality when results of scores are tied to the professional advancement of educators. Assessment, both formative and summative, must be linked to the goals teachers are being asked to achieve. The assessment of student understanding can be enhanced by the use of appropriate assessment tools and methods, such as portfolios, group projects, and authentic problem solving. However, students and parents alike may find these forms unfamiliar to the traditional assessment formula. Teachers need support from administration, school boards, and professional groups to help students and parents understand the value of using such approaches to enhance student learning and improve instruction.

How will "Professional Development Standards" help? Teachers, educators, and other members of the technology teaching profession need to know and use "Professional Development Standards" (chapter 4) of *AETL*. They need to be aware of the aspects of teaching technology that combine technological and pedagogical knowledge. The technology teaching profession must be as adaptable as the field of technology. It must be adaptable to changing curricula, practices, and laboratory-classroom experiences. It should incorporate new knowledge of how students effectively learn technology. Teacher preparation is the cornerstone for grooming teachers to teach technology, yet, as good as many technology teacher preparation programs are, they only provide teacher candidates with a small part of what they need to know and be able to do throughout their professional careers. In-service programs must be readily available to provide existing teachers with needed assistance and preparation for implementing *STL* and *AETL*, incorporating new technological topics and adjusting pedagogical practices to meet the needs of students and how they learn technology. Some technology teachers work in relative isolation, with little support for innovation or change and few incentives to improve their practice. Some of the best practices for teaching become apparent when teachers reflect on their teaching practices and share information with their colleagues. When teachers have time to work with colleagues to plan curricula, have time to make changes in pedagogy to meet the needs of students, and have time for personal reflection, they are better equipped to enhance their instruction and help students learn technology. Too often, the necessity for change is placed on the shoulders of teachers, and no support is provided. Subsequently, teachers are blamed when goals and objectives are not met as expected. A system-wide method of providing teachers with resources and support mechanisms needs to be in place to enable professional growth.

Additionally, school districts, states/provinces/regions, and teacher preparation institutions must be more proactive in recruiting new technology teachers. School districts should identify exemplary students of technology in middle or high schools who have the potential of becoming excellent technology teachers and encourage them to pursue the necessary education.

Are learning environments, instructional strategies and materials, curricula, textbooks, and other materials chosen with the vision of technological literacy in mind and reflective of "Program Standards?" The process of designing and constructing technology programs presents challenges for teachers and administrators. The choice of equipment, instructional materials, and other resources can be controversial and sometimes daunting. Technology teachers need time to prepare to work in a standards-based environment, and they need time to "live" with new curricula to understand the new environment's strengths and weaknesses. By having this time, teachers are able to design high-quality units and lessons that enable them to teach effectively in a variety of contexts. The design, selection, and construction of technology programs needs to be a collaborative process that is thoughtful, informative, and interactive, with all parties involved in the delivery of the program, including administrators, teachers, and teacher support personnel. Likewise, teachers and administrators need to keep parents and communities apprised of program decisions. The community's agreed-upon goals, along with "Program Standards" (chapter 5) of *AETL* and the school, school district, or state/provincial/regional policies and procedures, are a rich resource for program input. Developers of programs should refer to current research on how students learn and how to know what students know and use the standards recommended in *STL* and *AETL* as guides when making decisions.

Conclusion

STL and *AETL* both incorporate immediate and long-range goals for the study of technology. These two documents together lay the foundation for an ambitious but attainable set of expectations. Educators, families, policymakers, and others can use the recommendations in these two documents to guide the decisions they make in everything from reforming laboratory-classroom practices to establishing school, school district, or state/provincial/regional programs for the study of technology. Achieving these standards requires clear goals and the active participation of all concerned. Realizing the vision of *STL* and *AETL* requires standards-based content, student assessment that is aligned with curricular goals, enhanced preparation for teachers and opportunities for teacher professional growth, and programs for the study of technology that embrace high-quality instructional materials and facilities. The task ahead is difficult, but it is one that should be embraced and approached with the understanding that it can be done. Now is the time for all good professionals who teach technology to come together to see the vision come alive for the good of all students and the future.

STL and *AETL* both incorporate immediate and long-range goals for the study of technology. These two documents together lay the foundation for an ambitious but attainable set of expectations.

Now is the time for all good professionals who teach technology to come together to see the vision come alive for the good of all students and the future.

Advancing Excellence in Technological Literacy: *Student Assessment, Professional Development, and Program Standards*

APPENDICES

A-H

Advancing Excellence in Technological Literacy: Student Assessment, Professional Development, and Program Standards

History of Technology for All Americans Project

*A*dvancing Excellence in Technological Literacy: Student Assessment, Professional Development, and Program Standards *(AETL)* is the third and final phase of the Technology for All Americans Project (TfAAP), which was created by the International Technology Education Association (ITEA) and funded by the National Science Foundation (NSF) and the National Aeronautics and Space Administration (NASA). Development and refinement of *AETL* took place over three years (2000–2003) and involved hundreds of experts in the fields of technology, mathematics, science, engineering, and other disciplines. Their input was attained through various methods, including hearings, Web-based electronic document review, and individual reviews through the mail and in person.

The standards in *AETL* address student assessment, professional development, and program enhancement. The TfAAP Advisory Group provided valuable counsel to the project staff. These people have backgrounds in standards creation as well as infusion and implementation of standards across disciplines. Their support has sustained the vision of ITEA and TfAAP that all students can and need to become technologically literate. The TfAAP Standards Writing Team provided detailed input in fashioning the initial draft of *AETL*, and their continued review and input have added strength and quality to the final document. Three formal drafts of *AETL* were developed and reviewed before a final draft was prepared in autumn 2002.

The standards in *AETL* are based on *Standards for Technological Literacy: Content for the Study of Technology (STL)*, which was developed by TfAAP for ITEA from 1996–2000. In addition to developing *AETL* in 2000–2003, TfAAP has devoted much of its time to

TfAAP Standards Writing Team

implementing *STL*. Six Standards Specialists gave numerous presentations and workshops around the country on implementing *STL*.

Another goal of the project in Phase III was to gain a perspective on "What Americans Think About Technology." TfAAP partnered with the Gallup Organization to conduct a survey of 1,000 households in the United States. A committee of question writers provided valuable input, and Dr. Lowell Rose, Emeritus Executive Director of Phi Delta Kappa, served as a consultant to guide question development.

During preparation of *AETL*, the TfAAP staff worked closely with the Council for Technology Teacher Education (CTTE) and the National Council for Accreditation of Teacher Education (NCATE) to develop the *ITEA/CTTE/NCATE Curriculum Standards*. Many of the standards developed by ITEA/CTTE/NCATE are based on *STL* and "Professional Development Standards" (chapter 4) of *AETL*. The ITEA/CTTE/NCATE standards will be finalized in 2003 and made available to colleges and universities for use in accrediting teacher preparation programs in the United States.

Timeline for the Technology for All Americans Project

Phase I (October 1994 – September 1996)

Technology for All Americans: A Rationale and Structure for the Study of Technology developed and published.

Phase II (October 1996 – September 2000)

Standards for Technological Literacy: Content for the Study of Technology developed and published.

Phase III (October 2000 – September 2003)

Advancing Excellence in Technological Literacy: Student Assessment, Professional Development, and Program Standards developed and published.

- February 5, 2000: Advisory Group meeting in Washington, DC.
- Fall 2000 – Spring 2001: Initial research on *AETL* standards by TfAAP staff.
- Fall 2000: Standards Specialists organized and trained.
- June 27 – July 1, 2000: Draft 1 of *AETL* developed by Standards Writing Team in Salt Lake City, UT.
- February 6–7, 2000: Gallup Poll question committee meeting in Chantilly, VA.
- August 31, 2001: Advisory Group meeting in Washington, DC.
- May – June, 2001: Gallup survey conducted.
- July – December, 2001: Fourteen national hearings on *AETL* Draft 1.
- October – November, 2001: Electronic document review of *AETL* Draft 1 via ITEA's Web page (16 focus groups plus additional individual reviews).
- July – November, 2001: Gallup Poll data analyzed and draft of report written.
- Fall 2000 – June 2002: Standards Specialists workshops and presentations.
- January 17, 2002: Release of Gallup Poll Report titled, "ITEA/Gallup Poll Reveals What Americans Think About Technology" at a National Academies symposium in Washington, DC.

- January – March, 2002: *AETL* Draft 1 input analyzed, and Draft 2 created.
- March, 2002: Three hearings at the ITEA Conference in Columbus, OH on *AETL* Draft 2.
- April, 2002: *AETL* Draft 2 mailed to focus groups and individuals for review.
- May – August, 2002: *AETL* Draft 2 input analyzed, and Draft 3 created.
- July, 2002: Five regional workshops on implementing *STL* were conducted by the Standards Specialists.
- September, 2002: Draft 3 of *AETL* mailed to reviewers for input.
- September, 2002: Advisory Group meeting in Washington, DC.
- October, 2002: Review of *AETL* standards and guidelines by Southeastern Technology Education Conference participants, Raleigh, NC.
- October – November, 2002: *AETL* Draft 3 input analyzed, and final draft created.
- November 2002 – January 2003: *AETL* layout and typesetting completed.
- January – February, 2003: *AETL* printed.
- February, 2003: Standards Specialists organize for *AETL* implementation, Raleigh, NC.
- March, 2003: *AETL* released at ITEA Conference in Nashville, TN.
- Spring 2003: Fourth and final Advisory Group meeting in Washington, DC.
- March – April, 2003: Continued dissemination of *AETL*.
- March – September, 2003: Standards Specialists and TfAAP staff continued *AETL* and *STL* implementation in various regions, states, and localities.

Acknowledgements

The following lists have been compiled as carefully as possible from our records. We apologize to anyone who was inadvertently omitted or whose name, title, or affiliation is incorrect. Inclusion on these lists does not imply endorsement of this document.

Technology for All Americans Project Staff

William E. Dugger, Jr., DTE, Director

Shelli Meade, Editor and Contributing Writer

Crystal Nichols, Editorial Assistant and Data Coordinator

Lisa Delany, Senior Research Associate and Contributing Writer

TfAAP staff generously supported each step of the development process. Also, special thanks to Pam Newberry and Jodie Altice, former staff members, for their enthusiasm and devotion to the project.

International Technology Education Association Staff

Kendall Starkweather, DTE, Executive Director

Leonard Sterry, Senior Curriculum Associate

Katie de la Paz, Communications/Publications Coordinator

Catherine James, Web Site/Computer Operations Coordinator

Phyllis Wittmann, Accountant

Kathie Cluff, Assistant Editor/Publications Specialist

Michelle Judd, Coordinator of Meeting Planning

Barbara Mongold, Publications Services Coordinator

Moira Wickes, Database Coordinator/Registrar

Lari Price, Member Services Coordinator

Dora Anderson, Advertising/Exhibits Coordinator

Sima Govani, Accounts Receivable Coordinator

International Technology Education Association Board of Directors

Michael Wright, DTE, President, Central Missouri State University, MO

George Willcox, President-Elect, Virginia Department of Education, VA

David McGee, DTE, Past-President, Haltom Middle School, TX

Kendall Starkweather, DTE, Executive Director, ITEA, VA

Larry Claussen, TECA Director, Wayne State College, NE

Chuck Linnell, TECC Director, Clemson University, SC

John Ritz, DTE, CTTE Director, Old Dominion University, VA

Cyril King, DTE, ITEA-CS Director, SE Education and Library Board, Northern Ireland

Steve Price, Region 1 Director, Riverdale High School, GA

Andy Stephenson, DTE, Region 2 Director, Scott County High School, KY

Ben Yates, DTE, Region 3 Director, Central Missouri State University, MO

Joseph Scarcella, Region 4 Director, California State University, San Bernardino, CA

Advancing Excellence in Technological Literacy: Student Assessment, Professional Development, and Program Standards

Advisory Group

Rodger Bybee, Executive Director, Biological Sciences Curriculum Study, CO

Rodney Custer, DTE, Chair, Department of Technology, Illinois State University, IL

Elsa Garmire, Professor of Engineering, Dartmouth College, NH

Gene Martin, Special Assistant to the Vice President of Academic Affairs for Extended Learning, Southwest Texas State University, TX

JoEllen Roseman, Executive Director, American Association for the Advancement of Science, Washington, DC

Linda Rosen, Senior Vice President, Education, National Alliance of Business, Washington, DC

James Rubillo, Executive Director, National Council of Teachers of Mathematics, VA

Gerald Wheeler, Executive Director, National Science Teachers Association, VA

Pat White, Executive Director, Triangle Coalition for Science and Technology Education, Washington, DC

Michael Wright, DTE, Coordinator of Technology and Occupational Education, Central Missouri State University, MO

Standards Team

Student Assessment

Rod Custer, DTE, Illinois State University, IL, Chair

Robert Wicklein, DTE, University of Georgia, GA, Recorder

Joseph D'Amico, Educational Research Service, VA

Richard Kimbell, Goldsmiths College, University of London, United Kingdom

Mike Lindstrom, Anoka-Hennepin Educational Service Center, MN

Leonard Sterry, ITEA's Center to Advance the Teaching of Technology and Science, VA

Charles Pinder, Northern Kentucky University, KY

Steve Price, Riverdale High School, GA

James Rice, Marquette University, WI

Professional Development

Michael Daugherty, Illinois State University, IL, Chair

Anna Sumner, Westside Middle School, NE, Recorder

Marie Hoepfl, Appalachian State University, NC

Ethan Lipton, California State University, Los Angeles, CA

Pamela Matthews, National Education Association, Washington, DC

Diana Rigden, Council for Basic Education, Washington, DC

Anthony Schwaller, DTE, St. Cloud State University, MN

Jack Wescott, DTE, Ball State University, IN

Jane Wheeler, Monte Vista Elementary School, CA

Program

Mark Wilson, North Dakota Vocational and Technical Education, ND, Chair

Pat Foster, Central Connecticut State University, CT, Recorder

Barry Burke, DTE, Montgomery County Public Schools, MD

David Bouvier, DTE, Framingham Public Schools, MA

Michael De Miranda, Colorado State University, CO

Joan Haas, Conway Middle School, FL

Steve Shumway, Brigham Young University, UT

Doug Wagner, Manatee County Schools, FL

Gary Wynn, DTE, Greenfield-Central High School, IN

Standards Specialists

Elazer Barnette, North Carolina Agricultural and Technical State University, NC

Barry Burke, DTE, Montgomery County Public Schools, MD

Michael Daugherty, Illinois State University, IL

Ed Reeve, Utah State University, UT

Steve Shumway, Brigham Young University, UT

Anna Sumner, Westside Middle School, NE

ITEA and TfAAP wish to thank the National Science Foundation (NSF) and the National Aeronautics and Space Administration (NASA) for their funding of Phase III of the project. Special appreciation is given to Gerhard Salinger of NSF and Frank Owens of NASA for their advice and input. We appreciate all the support and help provided to TfAAP by the late Pam Mountjoy of NASA; we miss her continued support and encouragement.

ITEA and TfAAP would like to express appreciation to Jill Russell for serving as our evaluator throughout Phase III.

Thanks also to Ed Scott and Tony Olivis at Circle Graphics for designing and laying out *AETL*. R.R. Donnelley & Sons Company printed the standards; special thanks to T.J. Beason for her patience in coordinating this process.

Special appreciation is given to Kendall Starkweather, Leonard Sterry, Katie de la Paz, and Kathie Cluff for their editorial help and advice on the overall document.

We would like to thank Julia Bussey for providing many of the photographs for this document. She and Shelli Meade made trips to various schools to take pictures of elementary and secondary school students working in laboratory-classrooms in the study of technology as well as educators and teacher candidates engaged in professional development.

Special appreciation is given to the following personnel at the schools listed below for allowing us to take photographs for *AETL*:

■ **Blacksburg Middle School, Blacksburg, VA**

Gary McCoy, Principal

Jeffrey Cichocki, Technology Teacher

■ **Hidden Valley Middle School, Roanoke County, VA**

Jerry Weddle, Technology Supervisor

David Blevins, Principal

Robert Warren, Technology Teacher

■ **Ottobine Elementary School, Dayton, VA**

Romana Pence, Principal

Bonnie Berry, Teacher (kindergarten)

■ **McGaheysville Elementary School, McGaheysville, VA**

Bill Rauss, Principal

Janis Detamore, Teacher (2nd and 5th grade)

■ **Virginia Polytechnic Institute and State University, Blacksburg, VA**

Mark Sanders, Associate Professor and Program Leader, Technology Education

James LaPorte, Associate Professor, Technology Education

Sharon Brusic, Assistant Professor, Technology Education

Julia Bussey, Doctoral Graduate Teaching Assistant

Doug Koch, Doctoral Graduate Teaching Assistant

Terri Varnado, Doctoral Graduate Teaching Assistant

Publications and Electronic Communications Unit, University Relations

■ **Virginia Technology Education Association Summer Conference 2002 Williamsburg, VA**

Bret Gunderson

Bruce Haan

Joan Haas

Jim Hahn

Carl Hall

Mark Haltom

Dave Halver

Jerry Hamm

John Hansen

Robert Hanson

Linda Harpine

Richard Harris

Jo Ann Hartge

Kelvin Hasch

Larry Hatch

Craig Haugsness

Bill Havice

Judy Hawthorn

W.J. Haynie

Richard Heard

Carolyn Helm

Gregory Hendricks

T.J. Hendrickson

John Hickey

Roger Hill

Sam Hines

Derrick Hintz

Marie Hoepfl

Harold Holley

Douglas Hotek

Daniel Householder

Thomas Hughes

Van Hughes

Jim Hulmes

Akbav Humayun

Paul Hunt

Patricia Hutchinson

Joseph Huttlin

Mohammed Isleem

William Jackson

Steve Jacobson

Courtney Jenkins

Kurt Jensen

Jerry Jewell

Charles Johnson

Haldane Johnson

Jody Johnson

Michael Johnson

Alister Jones

David Jurewicz

Jim Kale

Erv Kallstrom

Moses Kariuki

Tom Karns

Paul Kenney

Patricia Keydel

Kamaal Khazen

Alan Kinnaman

Ken Kline

Tony Korwin

Randolph Kowalik

Ernest Kozun, Jr.

John Kraljic

Z.B. Kremens

Thomas Kubicki

Gerald Kuhn

John Kvartek

Greg Laban

Henry Lacy

Keith Landin

James LaPorte

Sheila Larson

Brenda Lattanzi

Bruce J. Lavallee

Carl Leiterman

John Leith

Joseph Leogrande

James Levande

Everton Lewis

Donald Libeau

Tung-I Lin

Robert Lindemann

Lisa Lindner

Mike Lindstrom

Chuck Linnell

Ethan B. Lipton

Mike Livieri

Dorian Lobdell

Mark Lockhart

Franzie Loepp

Roger Lord

Mary Lorenz

Thomas Loudermilk

Gerald Lovedahl

Thomas Loveland

Joe Luciano

John Lucy

Peter Lund

Bethany Lupo

Brian Mabie

Ken Maguire

Mary Margosian

Marco Margotta

Gene Martin

Cathy Mason

Pamela Matthews

David J. Matuszak

Marianne Mayberry

Vignette Credits

Pages 28–29. Formative assessment: Using student feedback. Adapted from a vignette written by Anna Sumner, Technology Teacher, Westside Middle School, Omaha, NE.

Pages 33–35. Summative assessment: Student product development portfolio. Adapted from a vignette written by Mike Lindstrom, Assessment Facilitator, Anoka-Hennepin Educational Service Center, Coon Rapids, MN; and Joe Nelson, Technology Education Department Leader, Champlin Park High School, Champlin, MN.

Pages 50–51. Modeling professional practice. Adapted from a vignette written by Michael Daugherty, Professor, Illinois State University, Normal, IL.

Pages 54–55. K–12 curriculum integration workshop. Adapted from a vignette written by James Boe, Curriculum Development Specialist, Valley City State University, Valley City, ND.

Pages 65–67. Facilitating collaboration. Adapted from a vignette written by Donna Matteson, Assistant Professor, Oswego State University of New York, Oswego, NY.

Page 76. A transformation, not a reformation: The need for district-wide vision and stakeholder buy in. Adapted from a vignette written by W. David Greer, DTE, Program Director, Fort Worth Independent School District, Fort Worth, TX.

Page 85. Data-based decision making. Adapted from a vignette written by John M. Ritz, DTE, Professor, Old Dominion University, Norfolk, VA.

Pages 90–91. The study of technology: A cross-curricular perspective. Contributions by Bonnie B. Berry, Kindergarten Teacher, Ottobine Elementary School, Dayton, VA; Janis Detamore, 2nd Grade Teacher, McGaheysville Elementary School, McGaheysville, VA; Thomas Kaiser, Technology Education Teacher, Maine East High School, Park Ridge, IL; Melvin Robinson, Technology and Engineering Specialist, Utah State Office of Education, Salt Lake City, UT.

Advancing Excellence in Technological Literacy: Student Assessment, Professional Development, and Program Standards

Listing of *STL* Content Standards

The Nature of Technology

Standard 1.   Students will develop an understanding of the characteristics and scope of technology.

Standard 2.   Students will develop an understanding of the core concepts of technology.

Standard 3.   Students will develop an understanding of the relationships among technologies and the connections between technology and other fields of study.

Technology and Society

Standard 4.   Students will develop an understanding of the cultural, social, economic, and political effects of technology.

Standard 5.   Students will develop an understanding of the effects of technology on the environment.

Standard 6.   Students will develop an understanding of the role of society in the development and use of technology.

Standard 7.   Students will develop an understanding of the influence of technology on history.

Design

Standard 8.   Students will develop an understanding of the attributes of design.

Standard 9.   Students will develop an understanding of engineering design.

Standard 10.   Students will develop an understanding of the role of troubleshooting, research and development, invention and innovation, and experimentation in problem solving.

Abilities for a Technological World

Standard 11.   Students will develop the abilities to apply the design process.

Standard 12.   Students will develop the abilities to use and maintain technological products and systems.

Standard 13.   Students will develop the abilities to assess the impact of products and systems.

The Designed World

Standard 14.   Students will develop an understanding of and be able to select and use medical technologies.

Standard 15.   Students will develop an understanding of and be able to select and use agricultural and related biotechnologies.

Standard 16.   Students will develop an understanding of and be able to select and use energy and power technologies.

Standard 17.   Students will develop an understanding of and be able to select and use information and communication technologies.

Standard 18.   Students will develop an understanding of and be able to select and use transportation technologies.

Standard 19.   Students will develop an understanding of and be able to select and use manufacturing technologies.

Standard 20.   Students will develop an understanding of and be able to select and use construction technologies.

Listing of *AETL* Standards with Guidelines

STUDENT ASSESSMENT STANDARDS:

Standard A-1: Assessment of student learning will be consistent with *Standards for Technological Literacy: Content for the Study of Technology (STL).*

Guidelines for meeting Standard A-1 require that teachers consistently

A. Administer comprehensive planning and development across disciplines.
B. Incorporate comprehensive planning and development across grade levels.
C. Include cognitive learning elements for solving technological problems.
D. Include psychomotor learning elements for applying technology.
E. Guide student abilities to operate within the affective domain, utilizing perspective, empathy, and self assessment.

Standard A-2: Assessment of student learning will be explicitly matched to the intended purpose.

Guidelines for meeting Standard A-2 require that teachers consistently

A. Formulate a statement of purpose for assessment tools.
B. Identify and consider the intended audience in designing assessment tools and reporting assessment data.
C. Utilize fair and equitable student assessment methods.
D. Establish valid and reliable measurements that are reflective of classroom experiences.

Standard A-3: Assessment of student learning will be systematic and derived from research-based assessment principles.

Guidelines for meeting Standard A-3 require that teachers consistently

A. Remain current with research on student learning and assessment.
B. Devise a formative assessment plan.
C. Establish a summative assessment plan.
D. Facilitate enhancement of student learning.
E. Accommodate for student commonality and diversity.
F. Include students in the assessment process.

Standard A-4: Assessment of student learning will reflect practical contexts consistent with the nature of technology.

Guidelines for meeting Standard A-4 require that teachers consistently

A. Incorporate technological problem solving.
B. Include variety in technological content and performance-based methods.
C. Facilitate critical thinking and decision making.
D. Accommodate for modification to student assessment.
E. Utilize authentic assessment.

Standard A-5: Assessment of student learning will incorporate data collection for accountability, professional development, and program enhancement.

Guidelines for meeting Standard A-5 require that teachers consistently

A. Maintain data collection for accountability.
B. Use student assessment results to help guide professional development decisions.
C. Use student assessment results to help guide program enhancement decisions.

Advancing Excellence in Technological Literacy: Student Assessment, Professional Development, and Program Standards

PROFESSIONAL DEVELOPMENT STANDARDS:

Standard PD-1: Professional development will provide teachers with knowledge, abilities, and understanding consistent with *Standards for Technological Literacy: Content for the Study of Technology (STL)*.

Guidelines for meeting Standard PD-1 require that professional development providers consistently prepare teachers to

    A. Understand the nature of technology.
    B. Recognize the relationship between technology and society.
    C. Know the attributes of design.
    D. Develop abilities for a technological world.
    E. Develop proficiency in the designed world.

Standard PD-2: Professional development will provide teachers with educational perspectives on students as learners of technology.

Guidelines for meeting Standard PD-2 require that professional development providers consistently prepare teachers to

    A. Incorporate student commonality and diversity to enrich learning.
    B. Provide cognitive, psychomotor, and affective learning opportunities.
    C. Assist students in becoming effective learners.
    D. Conduct and use research on how students learn technology.

Standard PD-3: Professional development will prepare teachers to design and evaluate technology curricula and programs.

Guidelines for meeting Standard PD-3 require that professional development providers consistently prepare teachers to

    A. Design and evaluate curricula and programs that enable all students to attain technological literacy.
    B. Design and evaluate curricula and programs across disciplines.
    C. Design and evaluate curricula and programs across grade levels.
    D. Design and evaluate curricula and programs using multiple sources of information.

Standard PD-4: Professional development will prepare teachers to use instructional strategies that enhance technology teaching, student learning, and student assessment.

Guidelines for meeting Standard PD-4 require that professional development providers consistently prepare teachers to

    A. Coordinate instructional strategies with curricula.
    B. Incorporate educational (instructional) technology.
    C. Utilize student assessment.

Standard PD-5: Professional development will prepare teachers to design and manage learning environments that promote technological literacy.

Guidelines for meeting Standard PD-5 require that professional development providers consistently prepare teachers to

- **A.** Design and manage learning environments that operate with sufficient resources.
- **B.** Design and manage learning environments that encourage, motivate, and support student learning of technology.
- **C.** Design and manage learning environments that accommodate student commonality and diversity.
- **D.** Design and manage learning environments that reinforce student learning and teacher instruction.
- **E.** Design and manage learning environments that are safe, appropriately designed, and well maintained.
- **F.** Design and manage learning environments that are adaptable.

Standard PD-6: Professional development will prepare teachers to be responsible for their own continued professional growth.

Guidelines for meeting Standard PD-6 require that professional development providers consistently prepare teachers to

- **A.** Assume commitment to self assessment and responsibility for continuous professional growth.
- **B.** Establish a personal commitment to ethical behavior within the educational environment as well as in private life.
- **C.** Facilitate collaboration with others.
- **D.** Participate in professional organizations.
- **E.** Serve as advisors for technology student organizations.
- **F.** Provide leadership in education.

Standard PD-7: Professional development providers will plan, implement, and evaluate the pre-service and in-service education of teachers.

Guidelines for meeting Standard PD-7 require that professional development providers consistently

- **A.** Plan pre-service and in-service education for teachers.
- **B.** Model teaching practices that teachers will be expected to use in their laboratory-classrooms.
- **C.** Evaluate professional development to assure that the needs of teachers are being met.
- **D.** Support technology teacher preparation programs that are consistent with state/ provincial/regional and national/federal accrediting guidelines.
- **E.** Provide teacher preparation programs, leading to licensure, that are consistent with *AETL* and *STL*.
- **F.** Provide in-service activities to enhance teacher understanding of technological content, instruction, and assessment.
- **G.** Obtain regular funding for in-service professional development opportunities.
- **H.** Create and implement mentoring activities at both in-service and pre-service levels.

PROGRAM STANDARDS (FOR TEACHERS):

Standard P-1: Technology program development will be consistent with *Standards for Technological Literacy: Content for the Study of Technology (STL).*

Guidelines for meeting Standard P-1 require that the teacher(s) responsible for the technology program(s) consistently

- A. Align program content with *STL*.
- B. Align program content with school district, state/provincial/regional, and national/federal standards in other academic areas.
- C. Plan and develop the program across disciplines.
- D. Plan and develop the program across grade levels.
- E. Assure that the program incorporates suitable cognitive, psychomotor, and affective learning elements.
- F. Promote adaptability for program enhancement.

Standard P-2: Technology program implementation will facilitate technological literacy for all students.

Guidelines for meeting Standard P-2 require that the teacher(s) responsible for the technology program(s) consistently

- A. Provide instruction that is consistent with research on how students learn technology.
- B. Provide instruction that is designed to meet curricular goals and student needs.
- C. Design and implement curricula that enable all students to attain technological literacy.
- D. Develop student leadership opportunities.

Standard P-3: Technology program evaluation will ensure and facilitate technological literacy for all students.

Guidelines for meeting Standard P-3 require that the teacher(s) responsible for the technology program(s) consistently

- A. Develop and utilize evaluation that is consistent with standards and guidelines in "Program Standards."
- B. Implement and use systematic, continuous evaluation.
- C. Evaluate instruction on a regular basis.
- D. Plan for program revision.
- E. Accommodate for student commonality and diversity.
- F. Utilize effective student assessment.

Standard P-4: Technology program learning environments will facilitate technological literacy for all students.

Guidelines for meeting Standard P-4 require that the teacher(s) responsible for the technology program(s) consistently

- A. Create and manage learning environments that are supportive of student interactions and student abilities to question, inquire, design, invent, and innovate.
- B. Create and manage learning environments that are up-to-date and adaptable.
- C. Implement a written, comprehensive safety program.
- D. Promote student development of knowledge and abilities that provides for the safe application of appropriate technological tools, machines, materials, and processes.
- E. Verify that the number of students in the technology laboratory-classroom does not exceed its capacity.

Standard P-5: Technology program management will be provided by designated personnel at the school, school district, and state/provincial/regional levels.

Guidelines for meeting Standard P-5 require that the teacher(s) responsible for the management of the technology program(s) consistently

- A. Develop and use action plans based on *STL*.
- B. Maintain data collection for accountability.
- C. Market and promote the study of technology.

PROGRAM STANDARDS (FOR ADMINISTRATORS):

Standard P-1: Technology program development will be consistent with *Standards for Technological Literacy: Content for the Study of Technology (STL)*.

Guidelines for meeting Standard P-1 require that administrators responsible for establishing the cross-curricular technology program consistently

- **G.** Stipulate that content be aligned with *STL*.
- **H.** Mandate instruction in the study of technology as part of the core educational experience for all students.
- **I.** Advocate content that complements school district, state/provincial/regional, and national/federal standards in other academic areas.
- **J.** Assure that the study of technology occurs across disciplines.
- **K.** Assure that the study of technology occurs across grade levels.
- **L.** Promote adaptability to enhance the study of technology.

Standard P-2: Technology program implementation will facilitate technological literacy for all students.

Guidelines for meeting Standard P-2 require that administrators responsible for establishing the cross-curricular technology program consistently

- **E.** Employ licensed teachers to deliver technology content.
- **F.** Support sustained professional growth and development of all educators.
- **G.** Encourage instruction that is consistent with research on how students learn technology.
- **H.** Advocate instruction that is designed to meet curricular goals and student needs.
- **I.** Commit to the recruitment of technologically competent teachers.
- **J.** Encourage all teachers to develop student leadership opportunities.

Standard P-3: Technology program evaluation will ensure and facilitate technological literacy for all students.

Guidelines for meeting Standard P-3 require that administrators responsible for establishing the cross-curricular technology program consistently

- **G.** Assure that evaluation is consistent with standards and guidelines in "Program Standards."
- **H.** Employ systematic, continuous evaluation.
- **I.** Encourage evaluation of instruction on a regular basis.
- **J.** Plan for program revision.

Standard P-4: Technology program learning environments will facilitate technological literacy for all students.

Guidelines for meeting Standard P-4 require that administrators responsible for establishing the cross-curricular technology program consistently

- **F.** Provide learning environments that are designed to facilitate delivery of *STL* and satisfy "Program Standards."
- **G.** Provide learning environments that are safe, up-to-date, and adaptable.
- **H.** Ensure that the number of students in a dedicated technology laboratory-classroom does not exceed its capacity.
- **I.** Provide elementary school classrooms with adequate physical space for teaching technology.
- **J.** Provide dedicated technology laboratory-classrooms in middle and high schools with a minimum allotment of 100 square feet per pupil, inclusive of safe ancillary space.

Standard P-5: Technology program management will be provided by designated personnel at the school, school district, and state/provincial/regional levels.

Guidelines for meeting Standard P-5 require that administrators responsible for the management of the cross-curricular technology program consistently

- **D.** Develop and use action plans based on *STL*.
- **E.** Maintain data collection for accountability.
- **F.** Market and promote the study of technology.
- **G.** Provide funding, support, and resources to accomplish missions, goals, and curricular objectives.
- **H.** Align technology programs with state/provincial/regional accreditation systems.
- **I.** Establish articulated and integrated technology programs district wide.
- **J.** Establish and utilize a management system.
- **K.** Support professional technology organization engagement by teachers and management personnel.
- **L.** Provide resources and opportunities to support technology teachers and other content area teachers in the teaching and learning process.

Correlation Chart

To increase the usability of *Advancing Excellence in Technological Literacy (AETL)*, correlations within and between the standards in *AETL* and *STL* are identified in the chart that follows. Such referencing indicates direct relationships (red type) and indirect relationships (black type) within and between these sets of standards.

This chart represents the perspective of TfAAP staff, who have interacted with the standards from a visionary point of view. ITEA recognizes that other correlations are possible, and this chart is, by no means, intended to be all-inclusive. ITEA welcomes further study and research to develop a more comprehensive correlative chart with and between *AETL* and *STL* as well as standards in other disciplines.

Student Assessment Standards				
Standard / Guideline Identification	Refer to *Student Assessment Standard*	Refer to *Professional Development Standard*	Refer to *Program Standard*	Refer to *STL*
A-1: CONSISTENCY WITH *STL*				
Standard A-1:	A-2, A-3, A-4	PD-1, PD-3	P-1, P-3	
Guideline A:	A-2C, D	PD-1A – E PD-3A, B, D	P-1B, C, I, J P-3B	Standard 3
Guideline B:	A-2C, D	PD-1A – E PD-3A, C, D	P-1A, D, G, H, K P-3B	Standards 1–20
Guideline C:	A-2C, D A-4A, C	PD-1A – E PD-3A	P-1A, E, G	Standards 1–10 Standards 14–20
Guideline D:	A-2C, D A-4A, B	PD-1A – E PD-3A	P-1A, E, G	Standards 11–20
Guideline E:	A-2C, D A-4C	PD-1A – E PD-3A	P-1A, E, G	Standards 1–7 Standards 14–20
A-2: INTENDED PURPOSE				
Standard A-2:	A-1, A-3	PD-3	P-3	
Guideline A:	A-3B, C		P-3F	Standards 1–20
Guideline B:			P-3F	
Guideline C:	A-1A – E A-3B, C, E, F	PD-3D	P-3E, F	
Guideline D:	A-1A – E	PD-3D	P-3F	
A-3: RESEARCH-BASED ASSESSMENT PRINCIPLES				
Standard A-3:	A-1, A-2	PD-2, PD-3	P-3	Standards 1–20
Guideline A:		PD-2D PD-3D		
Guideline B:	A-2A, C	PD-3D	P-3B, C, H, I	
Guideline C:	A-2A, C	PD-3D	P-3B, H	
Guideline D:		PD-2A, C	P-3C, F, I	
Guideline E:	A-2C	PD-2A	P-3E	
Guideline F:	A-2C	PD-2C	P-3F	
A-4: PRACTICAL CONTEXTS				
Standard A-4:	A-1	PD-1, PD-3	P-1, P-3	
Guideline A:	A-1C, D	PD-1A – E PD-3A	P-1A, E, G	Standards 1–20
Guideline B:	A-1D	PD-1A – E PD-3A	P-1A, E, G	Standards 1–20
Guideline C:	A-1C, E	PD-1A – C, E PD-3A	P-1A, E, G	Standards 1–10 Standards 14–20
Guideline D:		PD-1A – E PD-3D	P-1F, L P-3D, J	
Guideline E:		PD-3A		
A-5: DATA COLLECTION				
Standard A-5:	A-1 – A-4	PD-3, PD-7	P-1 – P-5	
Guideline A:		PD-3A – D	P-3B, G, H	
Guideline B:		PD-7A, F		
Guideline C:		PD-3A – D	P-3B, D, G, H, J	

Advancing Excellence in Technological Literacy: Student Assessment, Professional Development, and Program Standards

Professional Development Standards

Standard / Guideline Identification	Refer to *Student Assessment Standard*	Refer to *Professional Development Standard*	Refer to *Program Standard*	Refer to *STL*
PD-1: CONSISTENCY WITH *STL*				
Standard PD-1:	A-1, A-4	PD-2 – PD-5	P-1	
Guideline A:	A-1A – E A-4A – C, D	PD-2B – D PD-3A – C PD-5B, F	P-1A, C – F	Standards 1–3
Guideline B:	A-1A – E A-4A – D	PD-2B – D PD-3A – C PD-5B, F	P-1A, C – F	Standards 4–7
Guideline C:	A-1A – E A-4A – D	PD-2B – D PD-3A – C PD-5B, F	P-1A, C – F	Standards 8–10
Guideline D:	A-1A – E A-4A, B, D	PD-2B – D PD-3A – C PD-5B, F	P-1A, C – F	Standards 11–13
Guideline E:	A-1A – E A-4A – D	PD-2B – D PD-3A – C PD-5B, F	P-1A, C – F	Standards 14–20
PD-2: STUDENTS AS LEARNERS				
Standard PD-2:	A-3	PD-1, PD-3–PD-5	P-2, P-4	
Guideline A:	A-3D, E			
Guideline B:		PD-1A – E PD-3A PD-4A, C PD-5B	P-2A, C P-4A, D	Standards 1–20
Guideline C:	A-3D, F	PD-1A – E PD-4A, C	P-2A, D	
Guideline D:	A-3A	PD-1A – E PD-3D	P-2A	
PD-3: CURRICULA AND PROGRAMS				
Standard PD-3:	A-1 – A-5	PD-1, PD-2	P-1 – P-5	
Guideline A:	A-1A – E A-4A – C, E A-5A, C	PD-1A – E PD-2B	P-1A, C – E P-2A, C P-3A – C, F P-4A, D	Standards 1–20
Guideline B:	A-1A A-5A, C	PD-1A – E	P-1B, C P-2C P-3A, B, F	Standard 3
Guideline C:	A-1B A-5A, C	PD-1A – E	P-1A, D P-2C P-3A, B, F	Standards to 1–20
Guideline D:	A-1A, B A-2C, D A-3A – C A-4D A-5A, C	PD-2D	P-1A, B, D P-3A, B, F P5-B	Standards 1–20
PD-4: INSTRUCTIONAL STRATEGIES				
Standard PD-4:		PD-1, PD-2	P-2	Standards 1–20
Guideline A:		PD-2B, C	P-2B	
Guideline B:				
Guideline C:		PD-2B, C		

Standard / Guideline Identification	Refer to *Student Assessment Standard*	Refer to *Professional Development Standard*	Refer to *Program Standard*	Refer to *STL*
PD-5: LEARNING ENVIRONMENTS				
Standard PD-5:		PD-1, PD-2	P-4	Standards 1–20
Guideline A:			P-4B	
Guideline B:		P-1A – E PD-2B	P-4A	
Guideline C:				
Guideline D:		PD-2C	P-4A	
Guideline E:			P-4C – E	
Guideline F:		PD-1A – E	P-4B	
PD-6: CONTINUED PROFESSIONAL GROWTH				
Standard PD-6:		PD-1 – PD-5		
Guideline A:				
Guideline B:				
Guideline C:				
Guideline D:				
Guideline E:				
Guideline F:				
PD-7: PRE-SERVICE AND IN-SERVICE				
Standard PD-7:	A-5	PD-1 – PD-6		
Guideline A:	A-5B			
Guideline B:				
Guideline C:				
Guideline D:				
Guideline E:				
Guideline F:	A-5B			
Guideline G:				
Guideline H:				

| Standard / Guideline Identification | Program Standards | | | Refer to *STL* |
	Refer to *Student Assessment Standard*	Refer to *Professional Development Standard*	Refer to *Program Standard*	
P-1: CONSISTENCY WITH *STL*				
Standard P-1:	A-1, A-4	PD-1, PD-3	P-2 – P-5	
Guideline A:	A-1A – E A-4A – C	PD-1A – E PD-3A, C, D	P-2B, C, H P-3F P-4A, F	Standards 1–20
Guideline B:	A-1A	PD-3B, D	P-2B, H P-3F	
Guideline C:	A-1A	PD-1A – E PD-3A, B	P-2C P-3B, F, H	Standard 3
Guideline D:	A-1B	PD-1A – E PD-3A, C, D	P-2C P-3B, F, H	Standards 1–20
Guideline E:	A-1C – E A-4A – C	PD-1A –E PD-3A	P-2A, C, G P-3F P-4A	Standards 1–20
Guideline F:	A-4D	PD-1A – E	P-3D, F, J P-4B, G	
Guideline G:	A-1B – E A-4A – C		P-2B, C, H P-4A, D	Standards 1–20
Guideline H:	A-1A, B		P-2C, E, I P-4A, D, I, J	
Guideline I:	A-1A		P-2B	
Guideline J:	A-1A		P-2C	Standards 3
Guideline K:	A-1B		P-2C	Standards 1–20
Guideline L:	A-4D		P-3D P-4B	
P-2: IMPLEMENTATION				
Standard P-2:		PD-2 – PD-4	P-1, P-4, P-5	
Guideline A:		PD-2B, C, D PD-3A PD-4A	P-1E P-4A	
Guideline B:			P-1A, B, G, I P-4F	Standards 1–20
Guideline C:		PD-2B PD-3A, B, C	P-1A, C, D, E, G, H, J, K P-4F, I, J	Standards 1–20
Guideline D:		PD-2C	P-5C, F	
Guideline E:			P-1H P-4I, J	
Guideline F:				
Guideline G:			P-1E P-4A	Standards 1–20
Guideline H:			P-1A, B, G	
Guideline I:			P-1H P-5C	
Guideline J:			P-5C	
P-3: EVALUATION				
Standard P-3:	A-1 – A-5	PD-3	P-1, P-5	Standards 1–20
Guideline A:		PD-3A, B, C, D	P-5B	
Guideline B:	A-1A, B A-3B, C A-5A, C	PD-3A, B, C, D	P-1C, D P-5B	
Guideline C:	A-3B, D	PD-3A	P-5B	

Standard / Guideline Identification	Refer to *Student Assessment Standard*	Refer to *Professional Development Standard*	Refer to *Program Standard*	Refer to *STL*
Guideline D:	A-4D A-5C		P-1F, L	
Guideline E:	A-2C A-3E			
Guideline F:	A-2A – D A-3F	PD-3A, B, C, D	P-1A – F P-5B	
Guideline G:	A-5A, C		P-5B, E	
Guideline H:	A-3B, C A-5A, C		P-1C, D P-5B, E	
Guideline I:	A-3B, D		P-5B, E	
Guideline J:	A-4D A-5C		P-1F	
P-4: LEARNING ENVIRONMENTS				
Standard P-4:		PD-2, PD-5	P-1, P-2, P-5	Standards 1–20
Guideline A:		PD-2B PD-3A PD-5B, D	P-1A, E, G, H P-2A, G	
Guideline B:		PD-5A, F	P-1F, L	
Guideline C:		PD-5E		
Guideline D:		PD-2B PD-3A PD-5E	P-1G, H	
Guideline E:		PD-5E		
Guideline F:			P-1A P-2B, C	Standards 1–20
Guideline G:			P-1F	
Guideline H:				
Guideline I:			P-1H P-2C	
Guideline J:			P-1H P-2C	
P-5: MANAGEMENT				
Standard P-5:	A-5	PD-3	P-1 – P-4	
Guideline A:				Standards 1–20
Guideline B:	A-5A, C	PD-3D	P-3A – C, F – I	
Guideline C:			P-2D, I, J	
Guideline D:				Standards 1–20
Guideline E:	A-5A, C		P-3G – I	
Guideline F:			P-2D	
Guideline G:				

References and Resources

Accreditation Board for Engineering and Technology. (2002). *2001 ABET accreditation yearbook: For accreditation cycle ended September 30, 2001*. Baltimore, MD: Author.

American Association for the Advancement of Science. (1993). *Benchmarks for science literacy*. New York: Oxford University Press: Author.

American Council on Industrial Arts Teacher Education. (1986). *Implementing technology education yearbook*. Encino, CA: Glencoe Publishing Co.

American Industrial Arts Association. (1985). *Standards for technology education programs*. South Holland, IL: The Goodheart-Willcox Company, Inc.

Biological Sciences Curriculum Study. (2000). *Making sense of integrated science: A guide for high schools*. Colorado Springs: Author.

Black, P, & Wiliam, D. (1998). Inside the black box: Raising standards through classroom assessment. *Phi Delta Kappan, 80*(2),139–48.

Bybee, R. (2000). Achieving technological literacy: A national imperative. *The Technology Teacher, 60*(1), 23-28.

Council of Chief State School Officers. (1987). *Interstate new teacher assessment and support consortium*. Retrieved November 11, 2002, from http://www.ccsso.org/intasc.html.

Custer, R. (1994). *Performance based education: Implementation handbook*. Columbia, MO: Instructional Materials Laboratory.

Daiber, R., Litherland, L., & Thode, T. (1991). Implementation of school-based technology education programs. In M. J. Dyrenfurth & M. R. Kozak (Eds.), *Technological literacy* (CTTE 40th yearbook, pp. 187–211). Peoria, IL: Glencoe Division, Macmillan/McGraw-Hill.

Danielson, C. (1996). *Enhancing professional practice: A framework for teaching*. Alexandria, VA: Association for Supervision and Curriculum Development.

Geography Education Standards Project. (1994). *Geography for life: National geography standards*. Washington, DC: National Geographic Society.

Gilberti, A.F. & Rouch, D.L. (Eds.). (1999). *Advancing professionalism in technology education* (CTTE 48th yearbook). Peoria, IL: Glencoe/McGraw Hill, Inc.

Guskey, T.R. (2000). *Evaluating professional development*. Thousand Oaks, CA: Corwin Press, Inc.

Hoff, D. J. (2000). Teachers examining student work to guide curriculum, instruction. *Education Week, 20*(13), 1,14. Retrieved November 7, 2002 from http://www.edweek.org/ew/ew_printstory.cfm?slug=13work.h20.

International Society for Technology in Education. (2002). *National educational technology standards*. Retrieved November 7, 2002 from http://cnets.iste.org/.

International Technology Education Association. (1996). *Technology for all Americans: A rationale and structure for the study of technology*. Reston, VA: Author.

International Technology Education Association. (2000a). *Standards for technological literacy: Content for the study of technology*. Reston, VA: Author.

International Technology Education Association. (2000b). *Teaching technology: Middle school, Strategies for standards-based instruction*. Reston, VA: Author.

International Technology Education Association. (2001a). *Exploring technology: A standards-based middle school model course guide*. Reston, VA: Author.

International Technology Education Association. (2001b). *Teaching technology: High school, Strategies for standards-based instruction*. Reston, VA: Author.

International Technology Education Association. (2002a). *Foundations of Technology: A standards-based high school model course guide*. Reston, VA: Author.

International Technology Education Association. (2002b). *Technology starters: A standards-based guide*. Reston, VA: Author.

International Technology Education Association. (2003). *Measuring progress: A guide to assessing students for technological literacy*. Reston, VA: Author.

International Technology Education Association, Council of Technology Teacher Educators, & National Council for Accreditation of Teacher Education (2003). *ITEA/CTTE/NCATE curriculum standards*. Reston, VA: International Technology Education Association.

Kimbell, R. (1997). *Assessing technology: International trends in curriculum and assessment.* Philadelphia: Open University Press.

Linn, R. L. (2000). Assessments and accountability. *Educational Researcher, 29*(2), 4–14.

Loucks-Horsley, S., Hewson, P.W., Love, N., & Stiles, K.E. (1998). *Designing professional development for teachers of science and mathematics* (The National Institute for Science Education). Thousand Oaks, CA: Corwin Press, Inc.

Loucks-Horsley, S., & Matsumoto, C. (1999). Research on professional development for teachers of mathematics and science: The state of the scene. *School Science and Mathematics, 99*(5), 258–268.

Martin, E.E., (Ed.). (2000). *Technology education for the 21st century* (CTTE 49th yearbook). Peoria, IL: Glencoe/McGraw Hill, Inc.

Marzano, R.J., Rickering, D.J., & Pollack, J.E. (2001). *Classroom instruction that works: Research-based strategies for increasing student achievement.* Alexandria, VA: Association for Supervision and Curriculum Development.

McGourty, J. & DeMeuse, K.P. (2001). *The team developer: An assessment and skill building program.* New York: John Wiley and Sons.

Meyer, S. (2000) *Assessment strategies for standards for technological literacy: Content for the study of technology* [Electronic Monograph]. Reston, VA: International Technology Education Association.

Minnesota Department of Children, Families, & Learning. (1997). *Proposed permanent rules relating to the graduation rule, profile of learning.* St. Paul, MN: Author.

Moskal. B. M., & Leydens, J. A. (2000). Scoring rubric development: Validity and reliability. *Practical assessment, research, and evaluation.* Retrieved November 11, 2002, from http://ericae.net/pare/getvn.asp?v=7&n=10.

National Academy of Engineering & National Research Council. (2002). *Technically speaking: Why all Americans need to know more about technology* (A. Pearson & T. Young, Eds.). Washington, DC: National Academy Press.

National Association of State Boards of Education. (2000). Assessing the state of state assessments. In *The State Education Standard, 1,* 3–52.

National Board of Professional Teaching Standards. (2001). *National board standards and certificates.* Washington, DC: Author.

National Business Education Association. (2000). *Assessment in business education yearbook, 38.* Reston, VA: Author.

National Council for Accreditation of Teacher Education. (2000). *Professional standards for the accreditation of schools, colleges, and departments of education.* Washington, DC: Author.

National Council for History Standards. (1996). *National standards for history.* Los Angeles, CA: National Center for History in the Schools.

National Council of Teachers of English. (1996). *Standards for the English language arts.* Urbana, IL: International Reading Association and the National Council of Teachers of English.

National Council of Teachers of Mathematics. (1991). *Professional standards for teaching mathematics.* Reston, VA: Author.

National Council of Teachers of Mathematics. (1995). *Assessment standards for school mathematics.* Reston, VA: Author.

National Council of Teachers of Mathematics. (2000). *Principles and standards for school mathematics.* Reston, VA: Author.

National Education Goal Panel. (1997). *Implementing academic standards.* Papers commissioned by the National Education Goals Panel. Retrieved November 11, 2002, from http://www.negp.gov/page1%2D13%2D5.htm.

National Research Council. (1996). *National science education standards.* Washington, DC: National Academy Press.

National Research Council. (1999). *Designing mathematics or science curriculum programs: A guide for using mathematics and science education standards.* Washington, DC: National Academy Press.

National Research Council. (1999). *How people learn: Bridging research and practice* (M.S. Donovan, J.D. Bransford, & J.W. Pellegrino, Eds.). Washington, DC: National Academy Press.

National Research Council. (2000). *How people learn: Brain, mind, experience, and school* (J.D. Bransford, A.L. Brown, & R.R. Cocking, Eds.). Washington, DC: National Academy Press.

National Research Council. (2001a). *Educating teachers of science, mathematics, and technology.* Washington, DC: National Academy Press.

National Research Council. (2001b). *Knowing what students know: The science and design of educational assessment.* (J. Pellegrino, N. Chudowsky, & R. Glaser, Eds.). Washington, DC: National Academy Press.

National Staff Development Council. (2001). *Standards for staff development*. Retrieved November 22, 2002, from http://www.nsdc.org/library/standards2001.html.

Newberry, P. (2001). Technology education in the U.S.: A status report. *The Technology Teacher, 61* (1), 8–12. Retrieved April 4, 2002, from http://www.iteawww.org/.

Reed, W.C. & Ritz, J.M. (2000) *Design for the future: Strategic planning for technology educators*. [Electronic Monograph]. Reston, VA: International Technology Education Association.

Rider, B.L. (Ed.). (1998) *Diversity in technology education* (CTTE 47th yearbook). Peoria, IL: Glencoe/McGraw Hill, Inc.

Ritz, J.M., Israel, E.N., & Dugger, W.E. (Eds.). (2002). *Standards for technological literacy: The role of teacher education* (CTTE 51st yearbook). Peoria, IL: Glencoe/McGraw Hill, Inc.

Rose, L.C., & Dugger, W.E. (2002). *ITEA/Gallup poll reveals what Americans think about technology*. Reston, VA: International Technology Education Association.

Schmoker, M. & Marzano, R. J. (1999). Realizing the promise of standards-based education. *Educational Leadership, 56*, 17–21.

Schwaller, A.E. (2000). Knowing where you are going! In G. Eugene Martin (Ed.), *Technology education for the 21st century* (CTTE 49th yearbook, pp. 189–193). New York: Glencoe McGraw-Hill.

Snyder, J.F., & Hales, J.A. (Eds.). (1986). *Jackson's Mill Industrial Arts Curriculum Theory*. Muncie, IN: Center for Implementing Technology Education, Department of Industry and Technology, Ball State University.

Sparks, D. (1997). Reforming teaching and reforming staff development: An interview with Susan Loucks-Horsley. *Journal of Staff Development, 18*, 20–23.

U.S. Commission on National Security/21st Century. (2001). *Road map for national security: Imperative for change*. Retrieved April 4, 2002, from http://www.nssg.gov/PhaseIIIFR.pdf.

Wiggins, G., & McTighe, J. (1998). *Understanding by design*. Alexandria, VA: Association for Supervision and Curriculum Development.

Glossary

The terms defined and described in this glossary apply specifically to *Advancing Excellence in Technological Literacy: Student Assessment, Professional Development, and Program Standards (AETL)*. These terms may have broader meanings in different contexts.

Some Acronyms Used in this Publication

AAAS	American Association for the Advancement of Science.
ABET	Accreditation Board for Engineering and Technology.
ACIATE	American Council on Industrial Arts Teacher Education.
ACTE	Association for Career and Technical Education.
AETL	*Advancing Excellence in Technological Literacy: Student Assessment, Professional Development, and Program Standards.*
ASCD	Association for Supervision and Curriculum Development.
ASME	American Society of Mechanical Engineers.
BSCS	Biological Sciences Curriculum Study.
CATTS	Center to Advance the Teaching of Technology and Science.
CTTE	Council on Technology Teacher Education.
GESP	Geography Education Standards Project.
IDSA	Industrial Designers Society of America.
IEEE	Institute of Electrical and Electronic Engineers.
ISTE	International Society for Technology in Education.

ITEA	International Technology Education Association.
ITEA-CS	International Technology Education Association-Council of Supervisors.
JETS	Junior Engineering Technical Society.
NAE	National Academy of Engineering.
NAS	National Academy of Sciences.
NASA	National Aeronautics and Space Administration.
NCATE	National Council for Accreditation of Teacher Education.
NCHS	National Council of History Standards.
NCTE	National Council of Teachers of English.
NCTM	National Council of Teachers of Mathematics.
NRC	National Research Council.
NSF	National Science Foundation.
NSTA	National Science Teachers Association.
STL	*Standards for Technological Literacy: Content for the Study of Technology.*
TECA	Technology Education Collegiate Association.
TECC	Technology Education Children's Council.
TfAAP	Technology for All Americans Project (ITEA).
TSA	Technology Student Association.

General Glossary Terms

Ability — The capacity to demonstrate the application of knowledge and skills.

Accountability — The quality of being held answerable or responsible for, which may make one liable to being called to account.

Accreditation — A system designed to attest to the act of accrediting or the state of being accredited. An accreditation system would involve the approval of an institution of learning as meeting a prescribed standard or standards through a review board.

Across disciplines — Inclusive of all content area classrooms as appropriate to develop technological literacy.

Across grade levels — Inclusive of all grades specified in the identified levels of an institution of learning, such as across grades kindergarten through twelve for public school.

Action plan — A management strategy that includes program mission statements, goals, short- and long-range strategic planning, organization, evaluation, and responsibilities.

Advancing Excellence in Technological Literacy: Student Assessment, Professional Development, and Program Standards

Adequate — Sufficient to satisfy a requirement or meet a need as identified in a standard.

Administrators — Those professionals who manage any aspect of the educational system, including supervisors or teachers as appropriate.

Advisory committee — An organized body comprised of informed and qualified individuals with a specified responsibility to give advice in the development of an idea or process. Members may include parents, business and industry personnel, local engineers, technologists, and interested citizens.

Affective — Relating to, arising from, or influencing feelings or emotions.

Alternative licensure — Licensure obtained through means other than a traditional undergraduate teacher preparation program.

Ancillary space — Adequate, safe, and convenient storage that supplements laboratory-classroom space.

Application — Putting general knowledge and skills to specific use.

Articulation/Articulated — A planned sequence of curricula and course offerings from Grades K–12. The planned sequence may involve looking at course offerings across grade levels (vertical articulation) or the curriculum at a single grade level (horizontal articulation).

Assessment principles — The basic truths, laws, or assumptions held in the use of assessment. The assessment principles that are in current use should enhance student learning; provide coherency of programs and courses; identify expectations; ensure developmental appropriateness, and be barrier-free.

Attributes of design — Design characteristics, which specify that design be purposeful, based on certain requirements, systematic, iterative, creative, and involve many possible solutions.

Authentic assessment — An assessment method that directly examines student performance on tasks that are directly related to what is considered worthy and necessary for developing technological literacy. Traditional assessment, by contrast, relies on indirect or stand-in tasks or questions that are more efficient and simplistic than they are helpful in determining what students actually know and can do.

Barrier-free — Safely accessible for all students, regardless of and with consideration given to student interests, cultures, abilities, socio-economic backgrounds, and special needs.

Best practices — What works and does not work in the laboratory-classroom.

Brainstorming — A method of shared problem solving in which all members of a group spontaneously and in unrestrained discussion generate ideas.

Checklist — An evaluative tool, which could be in many forms, from a simple listing to a formal quarterly report of progress.

Class size — The number of students designated to participate simultaneously as a group.

Co-curricular — The part of student educational experience that exists in conjunction with the academic setting but also outside of it.

Cognitive — 1. Having a basis in or being reducible to empirical, factual knowledge. 2. A teaching method that recognizes the close relationship between what is known and what is to be learned. The teaching proceeds to build on the student's knowledge base by helping the student associate new material with something that is familiar.

Collaboration — A cooperative relationship that enables goals to be accomplished more effectively and comprehensively than by individual efforts.

Communicate — To exchange thoughts and ideas.

Constituent — A person or entity that patronizes, supports, or offers representation.

Context/Contextual — The circumstances in which an event occurs; a setting.

Continuous — Uninterrupted in time, sequence, substance, or extent.

Continuous-improvement model — The process of identifying educational goals; implementing strategies designed to achieve those goals; collecting data; analyzing the data in light of the goals and strategies; making changes; and continuing the cycle.

Control — An arrangement of chemical, electronic, electrical, and mechanical components that commands or directs the management of a system.

Core concepts — A set of ideas that make up the basis for the study of technology. The core concepts of technology as identified in *STL* are systems, resources, requirements, optimization and trade-offs, processes, and controls.

Correlation — In *AETL*, it shows a relationship within or between the standards in *AETL* and *STL*.

Courses of study — A series of lessons, activities, projects, or lectures that last a specified period of time and are designed around a specified school subject.

Critical thinking — The ability to acquire information, analyze and evaluate it, and reach a conclusion or answer by using logic and reasoning skills.

Cross-curricular technology program — Everything that affects student attainment of technological literacy, including content, professional development, curricula, instruction, student assessment, and the learning environment, implemented across grade levels and disciplines. The cross-curricular technology program manages the study of technology in technology laboratory-classrooms and other content area classrooms.

Cultural context — The culture setting of beliefs, traditions, habits, and values controlling the behavior of the majority of the people in a social-ethnic group. These include the people's ways of dealing with their problems of survival and existence as a continuing group.

Cumulative assessment — Assessment that is summative and usually occurs at the end of a unit, topic, project, or problem.

Curricula/Curriculum — Specification of the way content is delivered, including the structure, organization, balance, and presentation of content in the laboratory-classroom.

Curriculum development — The process of creating planned curriculum, pedagogy, instruction, and presentation modes.

Design — An iterative decision-making process that produces plans by which resources are converted into products or systems that meet human needs and wants, or solve problems.

Developmentally appropriate — Intended to match the needs of students in the areas of cognition, physical activity, emotional growth, and social adjustment.

Discipline — A specified realm of content.

Dynamic — Ever changing and evolving.

Educational (instructional) technology — The use of technological developments, such as computers, audio-visual equipment, and mass media, as tools to enhance and optimize the teaching and learning environment in all school subjects, including technology education.

Educators — Those professionals involved in the teaching and learning process, including teachers and administrators.

Effective — Produces the desired results with efficiency.

Empathy — The ability to place oneself in another person's perspective in order to better understand that person's point of view. Empathy provides more complete understanding than sympathy.

Engineering — The profession of or work performed by an engineer. Engineering involves the knowledge of the mathematical and natural sciences (biological and physical) gained by study, experience, and practice that are applied with judgment and creativity to develop ways to utilize the materials and forces of nature for the benefit of mankind.

Environment — The circumstances or conditions that surround one in a setting, such as a laboratory-classroom.

Evaluation — Collection and processing of information and data to determine how well a design meets the requirements and to provide direction for improvements.

Experiment — 1. A controlled test or investigation. 2. Trying out new procedures, ideas, or activities.

Explicitly — Clearly stated, leaving no ambiguity, and consequently able to be understood and re-stated by others.

External review — Evaluation by a group outside of the academic setting that can provide an impartial review of the program for purposes of accountability and improvement.

Extra-curricular — The part of student educational experience that exists outside of the academic setting but complements it.

Federal — Pertaining to a centralized government, as in the United States.

Formalized assessment — Assessment that is strictly standardized to allow for accurate comparisons.

Formative assessment — Ongoing assessment in the classroom. It provides information to students and teachers to improve teaching and learning.

Goals — The expected end results. In standards-based education, this can be specifically applied to learning, instruction, student assessment, professional development, and program enhancement.

Group project — Specific organized work or research by two or more individuals who interact with and are influenced by each other.

Guided discovery — A form of instruction in which learning takes place with a limited amount of teacher direction, and students are required to work out basic principles for themselves.

Guideline — Specific requirement or enabler that identifies what needs to be done in order to meet a standard.

Hands-on — Experiences or activities that involve tacit doing as a means of acquiring,

or a complement to acquiring, knowledge and abilities.

Holistic — Emphasis of the whole, the overall, rather than analysis and separation into individual parts.

Human adaptive systems — Systems that exist within the human-made and natural world, including ideological, sociological, and technological systems.

Informal observation — An assessment method that requires the teacher to observe students at work and note how they interact, solve problems, and ask questions.

Innovate — To renew, alter, or introduce methods, ideas, procedures, or devices.

In-service — 1. A practicing educator. 2. Workshops, lectures, and other educational opportunities designed to keep practicing professionals abreast of the latest developments in their fields.

Instruction — The actual teaching process that the teacher employs to deliver the content to all students.

Integration — The process of bringing all parts together into a whole.

Invention — A new product, system, or process that has never existed before, created by study and experimentation.

Knowledge — 1. The body of truth, information, and principles acquired by mankind. 2. Interpreted information that can be used.

Laboratory-classroom — The environment in which student learning takes place related to the study of technology.

Large-scale assessment — An assessment tool or method that involves a large number of students, such as across a state/province/region or nation.

Leadership — Guidance, direction, and support.

Learning environment —Formal or informal location where learning takes place that consists of space, equipment, resources (including supplies and materials), and safety and health requirements.

Local — 1. The individual school. 2. The environment defined by the administrative duties of a legally administered public agency within a state or province.

Long-range planning — Planning that spans weeks, months, or even years and may not commence until sometime in the future.

Macrosystem — A comprehensive, all-inclusive system.

Manageable class size — The number of students that (a) designated teacher(s) is/are able to most effectively and safely guide, direct, and instruct.

Manageable teacher schedule — A daily, weekly, monthly, semester, and term itinerary that allows teachers to accomplish goals for teaching and learning.

Notations — Within *AETL*, notations consist of definitions, tables, quotations, and correlations.

Mathematics — The study of abstract patterns and relationships that results in an exact language used to communicate about them.

Measurement — Collecting data in a quantifiable manner.

Mentor — A mentor possesses knowledge and experience and shares pertinent information, advice, and support while serving as a role model.

Meta-cognition — Learners reflecting upon their own process of thinking and learning.

Mission — Organized goals and strategies for realizing goals that could be articulated in a mission statement.

Model — A visual, mathematical, or three-dimensional representation in detail of an object or design, often smaller than the original. A model is often used to test ideas, make changes to a design, and to learn more about what would happen to a similar, real object.

Modeling — The act of creating a model.

Modular environments — Areas that, by design, allow for flexibility, as they can be arranged in a variety of ways to suit the purpose of the specific activity or lesson.

Narrative — Within *AETL*, narratives give the explanation of what is included in standards and guidelines.

National — Pertaining to the geographical extent of a centralized government, but not controlled by that single, centralized governing body.

Objective — A specific item or procedure that meets a designated goal.

Optimization — An act, process, or methodology used to make a design or system as effective or functional as possible within the given criteria and constraints.

Paper-and-pencil test — An assessment method that involves the use of questions that are typically answered in a timed setting using paper and pencil.

Pedagogical — Of or relating to the deliberately applied science/art, methodologies, and strategies of teaching.

Peer assessment — An assessment method that involves the use of feedback from one student to another student, both students being of similar standing (grade level).

Performance — A demonstration of student-applied knowledge and abilities, usually by presenting students with a task or project and then observing, interviewing, and evaluating their solutions and products to assess what they actually know and can do.

Performance-based method — A lesson or an activity that is designed to include performances that involve students in the application of their knowledge.

Perspective — An individual point of view based on experience.

Policymakers — 1. Those representatives inside the educational, public, and governmental system who are responsible for public education at school, school district, state/provincial/regional, and national/federal levels. 2. Those individuals, businesses, or groups outside the public educational system who influence educational policy. This may include parents, clubs, organizations, businesses, political activists, and any number of other citizens or groups of citizens who, while not directly and legally responsible for creating educational policy, nevertheless influence educational policy.

Portfolio — Formal or informal, systematic, and organized collection of student work that includes results of research, successful and less successful ideas, notes on procedures, and data collected. A portfolio may be in many forms, from photographs depicting student growth and understanding to a specialized electronic journal showing work completed over a period of time.

Practical context — The everyday environment in which an event takes place.

Practices — The established applications of knowledge.

Pre-service — 1. A teacher candidate. 2. Undergraduate level education for those who intend to teach.

Principle — A basic truth, law, or assumption that is widely accepted and followed as a general rule or standard.

Problem solving — The process of understanding a problem, devising a plan, carrying out the plan, and evaluating the plan in order to solve a problem or meet a need or want.

Process — 1. Human activities used to create, invent, design, transform, produce, control, maintain, and use products or systems. 2. A systematic sequence of actions that combines resources to produce an output.

Product — A tangible artifact produced by means of either human or mechanical work, or by biological or chemical processes.

Professional — Of or relating to practicing one's occupation with skill, knowledge, dedication, and with a conscious accountability for one's actions.

Professional development — A continuous process of lifelong learning and growth that begins early in life, continues through the undergraduate, pre-service experience, and extends through the in-service years.

Professional development providers — Those who organize and/or deliver pre-service and in-service teacher education, including teacher educators, supervisors, and administrators.

Program — Everything that affects student learning, including content, professional development, curricula, instruction, student assessment, and the learning environment, implemented across grade levels.

Program permeability — The vision behind *AETL*, which calls on teachers, administrators, and policymakers to perpetuate interchange between elements of the program, including content, professional development, curricula, instruction, student assessment, and the learning environment, in all areas of learning.

Project — A teaching or assessment method used to enable students to apply their knowledge and abilities. These may take many forms and are limited by time, resources, and imagination.

Prototyping — The act of creating a prototype, such as an original type, form, or instance, that serves as a working model on which later stages are based or judged.

Provincial — Of or belonging to a province, as in the ten main administrative divisions of Canada.

Psychomotor — 1. Physical behavior that has a basis in mental processes. 2. A teaching method that involves both mental processes and physical movement.

Qualified teacher — An individual possessing the necessary knowledge and skills to effectively teach specified subject matter to students in specified grade levels.

Questioning — A technique of informal assessment and instruction, wherein the teacher guides the direction, understanding, and application of the information being taught through the use of questions and also attempts to identify student misconceptions and uses that information to adjust instruction.

Reliability — Capable of being relied on; dependable; may be repeated with consistent results.

Regional — The administrative boundaries of a legally administered public agency, which may be combined with all other regions.

Research — Systematic, scientific, documented study.

Resource — A thing needed to get a job done. In a technological system, the basic technological resources are: energy, capital, information, machines and tools, materials, people, and time.

Requirements — The parameters placed on the development of a product or system. The requirements include the safety needs, the physical laws that will limit the development of an idea, the available resources, the cultural norms, and the use of criteria and constraints.

Rote memorization/response — A response that is generated by memory alone, without understanding or thought.

Rubric — An assessment or evaluative device based on the identified criteria taken from the content standards. Points or words are assigned to each phrase or level of accomplishment. This method gives feedback to the students about their work in key categories, and it can be used to communicate student performance to parents and administrators.

School district — The administrative boundaries of a legally administered public agency within a locality or state/province/region.

Science — Understanding the natural world.

Self assessment/Self reflection — An assessment method that encourages individuals to evaluate themselves, for example, in terms of their learning or teaching.

Short-range planning — Planning for the immediate future and for a relatively short period of time; for example, the next day, week, or the rest of the grading period.

Simulation — A method of instruction that attempts to re-create real-life experiences.

Society — A community, nation, or broad grouping of people having common traditions, institutions, and collective activities and interests.

Space — 1. The continuous expanse beyond the earth's atmosphere, as in space exploration. 2. The area allotted for a specific purpose, as in classroom space.

Stakeholder — An individual or entity who has an interest in the success of a specific venture or program. Stakeholders may include teachers, administrators, school leaders, professional development providers, business and industry leaders, engineers, scientists, technologists, and others.

Standard — A written statement or statements about what is valued that can be used for making a judgment of quality.

State — A geographically bound level of government that, combined with all other states, comprise the totality of the nation, as in the U.S. In terms of education, state authorities, administrators, and policymakers refer to those that administer publicly maintained schools.

Strategic planning — A disciplined effort to produce fundamental decisions and actions that shape and guide what an organization is, what it does, and why it does it, with a focus on the future.

Stem statements — Introductory phrases in *AETL* that appear before guidelines to connect individual guidelines to the standard addressed. Stem statements should always be used when quoting individual guidelines.

Student assessment — A systematic, multi-step process of collecting evidence on student learning, understanding, and abilities and using that information to inform instruction and provide feedback to the learner, thereby enhancing student learning.

Student interview — An assessment method that includes a planned sequence of questions, similar to a job interview. Students are not given information, as the objective is to collect data on student knowledge and abilities at a certain point in time. In contrast, a student conference suggests a discussion, with both student and teacher idea-sharing taking place.

Student presentation/demonstration — An assessment method that involves student explanation and communication of their understanding of key ideas, concepts, and principles and abilities of processes, techniques, and skills.

Study of technology — Any formal or informal education about human innovation, change, or modification of the natural environment.

Summative assessment — Cumulative assessment that usually occurs at the end of a unit, topic, project, or problem. It identifies what students have learned and judges student performance against previously identified standards. Summative assessment is most often thought of as final exams, but it may also be a portfolio of student work.

Systems — Groups of interrelated components designed to collectively achieve a desired goal or goals.

Systems-oriented — Looking at a problem in its entirety; looking at the whole, as distinct from each of its parts or components, taking into account all of the variables and relating social and technological characteristics.

Tactile — Stimulation through the sense of touch.

Teacher candidate — An individual preparing to teach.

Teaching — The conscious effort to bring about learning in a manner that is clearly understood by the learner and likely to be successful.

Technological competency — What some people need to be prepared to be successful in a technical career.

Technological literacy — The ability to use, manage, assess, and understand technology.

Technology — The innovation, change, or modification of the natural environment to satisfy perceived human needs and wants.

Technology education — A school subject specifically designed to help students develop technological literacy.

Technology program — Everything that affects student attainment of technological literacy, including content, professional development, curricula, instruction, student assessment, and the learning environment, implemented across grade levels as a core subject of inherent value.

Test (e.g., multiple choice, true/false, essay, etc.) — 1. A method for collecting data. 2. A procedure for critical evaluation.

Trade-off — An exchange of one thing in return for another; especially relinquishment of one benefit or advantage for another regarded as more desirable.

Unit — An organized series of learning activities, lectures, projects, and other teaching strategies that focuses on a specific topic related to the curriculum as a whole.

Validity — Having or containing premises from which the conclusion may logically be derived, correctly inferred, or deduced.

Vignette — An illustration or literary "snapshot" that, in *AETL*, provides detailed examples of how standards can be put into practice.

Vision — A contemplative image of future promise and possibility articulated with the intention to inspire others.

Workstation — A student work area, including all the components that occupy the space, such as furniture and equipment.

Index

Note: Page numbers followed by *f* denote reference to the figure on the identified page number. Page numbers followed by *t* denote reference to the table on the page.

Funding
    for professional development, 64
    for technology programs, 94

G

*Geography for Life: National
    Geography Standards* (GESP),
    73, 75
Grade levels
    curricula and programs across, 49,
        73–74, 75
    student assessment across, 21
Guidelines
    architecture of, 7
    definition of, 7
    narrative of, 7

H

Higher education, teacher educator
    roles in, 99–100
Holistic approach, to student assess-
    ment, 30

I

Implementation, of technology pro-
    gram, 77–80
*Implementing Technology Education
    Yearbook* (ACIATE), 86
In-service professional development.
    See Professional development;
    Professional development
    standards
Industry, roles of, 101–102
Instruction, 58, 78, 79
    definition of, 15
    evaluation of, 82–83, 84
Instructional strategies, 52–53, 78
Instructional technology, 53, 78, 79,
    88
    definition of, 11
Intended purpose, of student assess-
    ment, 22–23
Interdisciplinary
    curricula and programs, 49,
        54–55, 73, 75
    student assessment, 21
International Technology Education
    Association (ITEA), 1, 7, 9,
        12, 90, 98, 102, 108, 109
    Board of Directors, 111
    Council of Supervisors (ITEA-CS),
        98
    staff, 111
ITEA. *See* International Technology
    Education Association
*ITEA/CTTE/NCATE Curriculum
    Standards,* 109

J

JETS. *See* Junior Engineering
    Technical Society

Junior Engineering Technical
    Society (JETS), 61, 78, 80, 93,
        94, 98

K

*Knowing What Students Know: The
    Science and Design of
    Educational Assessment* (NRC),
        18, 19, 24, 36

L

Laboratory-classroom. *See* Learning
    environment
Leadership
    of administrators, 95
    of students, 61, 78, 80
    of teachers, 61
Learners, students as, 45–46, 78, 79
    (*See also* Student learning)
Learning environment
    adaptability of, 58, 87, 88–89
    definition of, 15
    design of, 56–58, 87, 88
    number of students in, 88, 89
    physical space of, 89
    in professional development stan-
        dards, 56–58
    in program standards, 86–89
    resources in, 57, 86, 87, 88–89
    safety of, 58, 87, 88–89
    student commonality and diver-
        sity and, 57–58
    and student learning, 57, 58, 86
    and teacher instruction, 58, 86
    vignette of, 90–91
Learning, of students. *See* Student
    learning
Licensure
    professional development and, 64
    and teacher employment, 79

M

Management, of programs, 92–96
Mathematics, and technology, 13
Mentoring, 64
Modeling, of teaching practices, 63
    vignette of, 50–51
Museums, roles of, 102

N

Narrative
    of guidelines, 7
    of standards, 7
NAE. *See* National Academy of
    Engineering
NASA. *See* National Aeronautics
    and Space Administration
National Academy of Engineering
    (NAE), 10, 12, 13, 102
National Aeronautics and Space
    Administration (NASA), 1,
        108

*National Educational Technology
    Standards for Students* (ISTE),
        73, 75
National Research Council (NRC),
    10, 12, 18, 19, 24
National Science Education Standards
    (NRC), 10, 13, 73, 75
National Science Foundation (NSF),
    1, 9, 108
National standards, 73, 75
National Standards for History
    (NCHS), 73, 75
Notations, definition of, 7
NRC. *See* National Research
    Council
NSF. *See* National Science Foundation

P

Parent(s), roles of, 101
Performance-based assessment, 21, 31
Policymakers, roles of, 100
Portfolios, in student assessment,
    22, 25, 83
    vignette of, 33–35
Pre-service professional develop-
    ment. *See* Professional develop-
    ment; Professional
    development standards
*Principles and Standards for School
    Mathematics* (NCTM), 73, 75
Problem solving
    in professional development,
        43–44
    in student assessment, 31
Professional development
    accountability in, 59–61
    and accreditation guidelines,
        63–64
    administrators and, 79
    continuous nature of, 40–41,
        59–61
    definition of, 4, 14, 40
    design in, 43–44
    evaluation of, 62, 63
    funding for, 64
    and licensure, 64
    mentoring and, 64
    modeling of teaching practices in,
        63
    problem solving in, 43–44
    and program permeability, 41
    and student assessment, 36–37
    teacher responsibility for, 59–61
Professional development standards,
    4–5, 4t, 39–67, 104, 122–123
    applications of, 40
    audiences for, 41
    correlations of, 128–129
    Standard PD-1 (consistency with
        STL), 42–44, 122
        correlations of, 42, 128
        guidelines for meeting, 43–44